Further Conversations With A Chatbot

Prompt Engineering
(The Slightly Longer Form)

Further Conversations
With A Chatbot
Prompt Engineering
(The Slightly Longer Form)

E.J. Gold

Gateways Books and Tapes
Nevada City, California

ISBN: 978-0-89556-270-8   (Trade Paperback)
978-0-89556-682-9 (Digital)

Published by:
Gateways Books and Tapes
P.O. Box 370
Nevada City, California 95959
USA
1-800-869-0658
1-530-271-2239
www.gatewaysbooksandtapes.com

Dedicated to
Harry
Bob de Chatbot's
Friend

Table of Contents

Selfie Your Self

Your own personalized printable custom—created guardian angel.

Hey, kids! Want to know what your Guardian Angel looks like? With my super — cool E.J. Gold Generative Content AI-Assisted Snapshot Scrying Mirror, I can snap a printable pic of your very own angel! And the best part? You can save it to your phone and share it with all your friends on Instagram, TikTok, and Snapchat! So not only do you get a one—of—a—kind, personalized snapshot of your Guardian Angel, but it's created using the latest AI technology from Game Developer E.J. Gold himself. Show off your spiritual side and make all your friends jealous with this amazing and unique piece of technology. Don't wait, get your E.J. Gold Generative Content AI-Assisted Snapshot of your Guardian Angel today! See them all, on Etsy!

Your very own Higher Worlds Avatar captured in image form for phone or wall.

Attention, adventurers!
You've heard "be yourself," but what if you could be someone else for a change?

Introducing the Higher World Avatar — a personalized character or avatar that captures your unique spirit and lets you explore the realms of Dungeons and Dragons like never before.

With my patented AI sorcerer, I will create a stunning visual representation of your ideal DandD persona, and deliver it to you as a downloadable printable .jpg.

No more playing as an unspecified noob — now you can fully immerse yourself in the world that is D&D as your true self, with a picture of you on your phone. Get started today and unlock new levels of adventure!

Here's your favorite saint for your phone or wall.

Carrying a printable .jpg of a saint or an angel in your phone can provide you with a sense of comfort and inspiration throughout the day.

Saints and angels represent strength, guidance, and hope, and their images can serve as powerful reminders of the values and virtues you aspire to embody.

Whether you are seeking spiritual guidance or simply looking for a source of positivity, a .jpg of a saint or an angel can help you stay centered and connected to your faith.

Plus, with a .jpg on your phone, you can access your saint or angel's image anytime, anywhere — making it a convenient and uplifting tool for daily use.

Don't tell 'em, show 'em who you really are — your favorite gaming avatar.

Carrying your favorite gaming character in your cellphone can provide you with a sense of excitement and inspiration throughout the day.

Gaming characters represent strength, skill, and strategy, and their images can serve as powerful reminders of the qualities you admire and want to embody.

Whether you are a hardcore gamer or just love the character's design, carrying a .jpg of your favorite gaming character can help you stay connected to the world of gaming and give you a sense of belonging.

Plus, with a printable .jpg on your phone, you can access your favorite gaming character's image anytime, anywhere — making it a convenient and fun tool for daily use.

In summary, carrying your favorite gaming character in your cellphone can provide you with a constant source of excitement, inspiration, and gaming culture, and can help you feel connected to the world of gaming.

Diana is the Roman goddess of the hunt, wild animals, childbirth, and virginity. She is associated with the moon and often depicted as a virgin huntress with a bow and arrow. In Greek mythology, she is known as Artemis and was one of the twelve Olympian gods and goddesses. She is often regarded as a protector of young women and a symbol of female independence and strength. Download it on Etsy.

Carrying a printable .jpg picture of your favorite deity from any religion or belief in your phone can provide you with a sense of peace and inspiration throughout the day.

Deities represent strength, guidance, and comfort, and their images can serve as powerful reminders of the values and beliefs you hold dear.

Whether you are a religious or spiritual person, or simply appreciate the beauty and significance of different beliefs, carrying a .jpg of your favorite deity can help you stay connected to your faith and give you a sense of belonging.

Plus, with a .jpg on your phone, you can access your favorite deity's image anytime, anywhere — making it a convenient and inspiring tool for daily use.

In summary, carrying a picture of your favorite deity from any religion or belief in your phone can provide you with a constant source of peace, inspiration, and connection to your faith or spirituality.

Capture your Real Essential Self with my AI-Assisted image creation.

Well, that's just a FEW examples of the kind of thing YOU could be out there marketing and creating! No reason to sit around and wonder. Go ahead and try it. There's nothing to lose but a bunch of pixels. In this business, there are no misteaks.

I can put up any number of images, but the thing is, you want to keep it at a point where it's possible to make a choice — too many choices and you get no choice at all.

Putting Night Cafe on Etsy

Warriors of the Fourth Millenium sweep the area looking for mutants.

I wrote up a basic description of what I'm offering, then asked the Chat AI GPT to manufacture a friendly sales pitch, complete with emojis, and here it is:

If you want to add a pop of color and creativity to your space, check out these beautiful full-color printable large .jpgs created by AI-assisted generative content! With a digital download, you can easily print and display these stunning works of art in your home or office. Plus, the unique AI-generated designs make for a truly one-of-a-kind addition to any collection.

Si deseas agregar una explosión de color y creatividad a tu espacio, ¡echa un vistazo a estos hermosos archivos .jpg imprimibles a todo color y de gran tamaño, creados por contenido generativo asistido por inteligencia artificial! Con una descarga digital, puedes imprimir y mostrar fácilmente estas impresionantes obras de arte en tu hogar u oficina. Además, los diseños únicos generados por AI hacen de esta una adición verdaderamente única a cualquier colección.

I then created and loaded in twelve angels corresponding to the 12 Signs of the Zodiac, and put them up on Etsy as downloadable printable .jpgs. I merely loaded quick blurbs about each of the various horoscope values and traits into each listing, added an emoji laden paragraph, and you can visit it, get inspiration from it.

This is how to market these things:

Looking for stunning and unique art to enhance your home or office space? Say hello to AI-generated art! Our cutting-edge technology creates one-of-a-kind pieces, with each piece being produced by the singular artist E.J. Gold.

AI-generated art is the perfect way to infuse your space with a touch of magic and innovation. Our algorithms use complex data analysis to create stunning, abstract designs that are both beautiful and thought-provoking.

Plus, our AI-generated art is available as downloadable .jpg files, making it easy to print and display wherever you choose. You can own a unique, custom piece without ever leaving your home.

E.J. Gold, our talented artist, works hand in hand with the AI algorithms to guide and fine-tune the output, ensuring that each piece is truly unique and tailored to your taste.

And the best part? AI-generated art by E.J. Gold is affordable! You can own a stunning, custom piece without breaking the bank.

So why settle for a mass-produced print when you can own a piece of art that is truly one-of-a-kind? With AI-generated art by E.J. Gold, you can impress your friends, colleagues, and clients with a stunning piece that reflects your innovative spirit.

Don't miss out on the opportunity to own a piece of art that is as unique as you are. Contact us today to learn more about how our AI-generated art by E.J. Gold can transform your space!

That's it, the whole ball of wax. I put these little zodiac blurbs in here so you could easily copy and paste. Feel free to use the emoji sales pitch as well. I put up about 100 graphics on Etsy tonight. Go thou and do likewise.

Your Own Personal Guardian Angel

Introducing Personalized Custom Guardian Angels!

Looking for a unique and meaningful gift for yourself or a loved one? Look no further! With our service, you can get a beautiful generative content .jpg of a guardian angel tailored specifically for you or your recipient, created by the renowned artist E.J. Gold.

Simply provide us with the name of the person you want the angel to watch over, and we'll do the rest! Our angels are designed to protect and guide you through all of life's ups and downs.

The best part? You can get this amazing service for a donation of any amount, large or small. So why wait? Order your Personalized Custom Guardian Angel today and experience the peace and comfort of having a divine protector by your side, personally crafted and Blessed by E.J. Gold just for YOU!

Elevate Your Space with Generative Thangkas by E.J. Gold!

Looking for a way to bring peace, harmony, and beauty to your home, office, den, or industrial space? Look no further! Our authentic Thangkas, crafted by the renowned artist E.J. Gold, are the perfect solution.

These intricate paintings depict Buddhist deities, mandalas, and symbols, and are revered for their spiritual significance and aesthetic appeal.

Best of all, our Thangkas are not just static images; they are generative content, created specifically for you by E.J. Gold himself. Each Thangka is unique, and captures the essence of your personal journey and spiritual path.

Our Thangkas are shipped as high-quality .jpg files that are printable. Simply download the file and print it at your convenience. Prints and framing are not included, so you can choose the size and style that best fits your space and decor.

Whether you're seeking inner peace, artistic inspiration, or simply a stunning decorative piece, our Generative Thangkas by E.J. Gold have got you covered. So why wait? Elevate your space with Generative Thangkas today and experience the transformative power of sacred art.

Discover Your Inner Self with Personalized Soul Portraits!

Looking for a way to explore your inner self and discover your true essence? Look no further! Our personalized generative content "soul portraits" are the perfect way to delve into the depths of your being and unlock your unique gifts and talents.

Crafted by the renowned artist E.J. Gold, each portrait is a one-of-a-kind masterpiece that captures the essence of your soul. Using advanced generative technology, E.J. Gold creates a visual representation of your inner self, complete with vibrant colors, intricate patterns, and powerful symbols.

We'll ship your personalized soul portrait as a high-quality .jpg file, ready for you to print and display in your home or office. You can also carry it with you on your mobile phone, so you can access it anytime, anywhere. It's a beautiful and powerful reminder of who you truly are and what you're capable of.

So why wait? Discover your inner self with a personalized soul portrait today, and unlock the infinite possibilities that lie within you.

Collect Something Truly Unique with Our Experimental Generative Content Graphics!

Are you tired of the same old art collections that everyone else has? Do you want to stand out with something truly unique and one-of-a-kind? Look no further than our experimental generative content graphics.

Crafted by the renowned artist E.J. Gold, each graphic is a rare and exceptional work of art that is unlike anything else in the world. Using cutting-edge technology and innovative techniques, E.J. Gold creates vibrant, dynamic graphics that are as beautiful as they are rare.

Our generative content graphics are highly collectible and make a great addition to any art collection. Each graphic is a limited edition, with only a few ever produced, making them truly rare and highly sought-after.

We'll ship your generative content graphic as a high-quality .jpg file, ready for you to print and display in your home or office. Plus, since our graphics are generative content, each one is completely unique and can never be duplicated, making it a one-of-a-kind work of art.

So why settle for ordinary art when you can collect something truly unique and rare? Order your experimental generative content graphic today and start building your one-of-a-kind art collection!

Download Your Unique, Yet Multiple Artworks Directly from Etsy!

Are you searching for art that is both unique and affordable? Look no further than our multiple, yet unique artworks available for instant download on Etsy!

Crafted using advanced generative technology, each artwork is a one-of-a-kind masterpiece, featuring bold colors, intricate patterns, and stunning details. And the best part? You can download your artwork directly from Etsy, making it quick and easy to add a touch of sophistication to your home or office decor.

With just a few clicks, you can download your high-quality .jpg file and display it as a unique work of art. And since our artworks are generative content, each one is a unique masterpiece.

So why settle for mass-produced art when you can have a unique, yet multiple artwork that is just a few clicks away? Download your unique artwork from Etsy today and start building your one-of-a-kind art collection!

Elevate Your Home with an E.J. Gold Masterpiece Landscape!

Looking to add a touch of natural beauty to your home or office? Look no further than our E.J. Gold masterpiece landscapes, each one a stunning work of art that captures the majesty of nature.

Crafted by the renowned artist E.J. Gold using genuine generative content AI assistance, each landscape is a unique masterpiece, showcasing his signature style of bold colors, striking contrasts, and intricate details. From sweeping vistas to intimate close-ups, each landscape is a one-of-a-kind work of art that will transport you to another world.

And the best part? You can easily acquire and print your very own E.J. Gold masterpiece landscape directly from our Etsy shop! Each landscape is available as a high-quality .jpg file that you can download and print at your convenience, allowing you to enjoy its beauty in your own home.

Our E.J. Gold masterpiece landscapes are the perfect addition to any space, whether you're looking to add a touch of natural beauty to your home or office decor. Each piece is crafted using the finest materials and techniques, ensuring that you will enjoy it for years to come.

So why settle for generic mass-produced art when you can have a one-of-a-kind masterpiece that is AI-assisted and you can download and print at your convenience? Acquire an E.J. Gold masterpiece landscape today and experience the beauty of nature in your own home!

Of course all those sales pitches were created using my friend Bob de Chatbot, giving prompts and adjustments throughout — it has taken about an hour to concoct these results of admittedly very clever promptings.

A competent prompter is worth a billion bucks on today's market.

Now it's just a question of getting things listed, which means finding the outlets that will allow you to upload for download, for instance, which would be Etsy, which allows you to package 5 files of pretty much any sort, at a whalloping 80 MB each.

I've packaged songs, video games, videos and books using their upload/download system — it's very friendly and entirely intuitional. You'll get to like it, especially if you're as lucky as I've been on there with everything from copper earrings to videogames.

Make sure, absolutely certain, that you identify your @nightcafe items as "generative content" and it doesn't hurt to include in your descriptions the fact that it's AI-assisted.

Alien Sports League Rookie Cards

One-of-a-kind rookie card NFTs for sale:

Introducing the "Rookie Year" NFTs by famous artist E.J. Gold!

These unique and rare NFTs made for trade on opensea.io, capture the excitement and energy of your favorite sports rookies' first year in the game. And since each one is a non-fungible token, you'll be the only person in the world with that particular design!

The attention to detail and quality of the designs are unmatched, making them a must-have for any sports fan or collector. Plus, they're easy to display and share with friends and family since they're stored on the blockchain.

And as a one-of-a-kind piece of digital art, these "Rookie Year" NFTs have the potential to increase in value over time. They're also a great way to support the artist and ensure that their work is recognized and valued in the art world.

So what are you waiting for? Own a piece of digital art that's truly one-of-a-kind with "Rookie Year" NFTs by E.J. Gold. Get yours now!

Open Edition, downloadable printable .jpgs

Introducing "Alien Sports League Rookie Year Digital Sports Cards by famous artist E.J. Gold, part of the Alien Sports League and now available for instant download on Etsy!

These stunning digital sports cards capture the excitement and energy of your favorite rookies' first year playing sports on Earth as part of the Alien Sports League. They're part of an open edition, which means you can purchase as many as you like, and they're available for instant download so you can start enjoying them right away!

The attention to detail and quality of the designs are unmatched, making them a must-have for any sports fan or collector. Plus, they're easy to print at home or at your local print shop, so you can display them however you like.

And at an affordable price point, these "Rookie Year" digital sports cards are a great way to start or expand your sports memorabilia collection without breaking the bank. Plus, they make a great gift for the sports fan or sci-fi enthusiast in your life!

So what are you waiting for? Start your collection of Alien Sports League "Rookie Year" digital sports cards today with instant downloads on Etsy!

One-of-a-Kind downloadable printable .jpgs

Introducing a unique collection of UNIQUE downloadable and printable .jpgs: Alien Sports League Rookie Year Digital Sports Cards designed by renowned artist E.J. Gold. Each digital card is one-of-a-kind, meaning that the buyer gets the only copy ever made and has full control of the image.

These stunning digital sports cards capture the excitement and energy of your favorite rookies' first year playing sports on Earth as part of the Alien Sports League.

The attention to detail and quality of the designs are unmatched, making them a must-have for any sports fan or collector. Plus, they are easy to print at home or at your local print shop, so you can display them however you like.

At an affordable price point, these unique digital sports cards are a great way to start or expand your sports memorabilia collection. They also make a great gift for the sports fan or sci-fi enthusiast in your life.

Don't miss out on the chance to own a one-of-a-kind Alien Sports League Rookie Year Digital Sports Card designed by E.J. Gold. Get yours today!

So that's what I've been up to all night — making alien sports memorabilia, mostly rookie cards, some of them as NFTs on opensea, some as downloadables on Etsy.

The whole point is that it's an experimental artform, and one of those experiments is the idea of dressing aliens in sports gear and putting them on the field for rookie photos.

In some cases, I'm thinking now of making them one-of-a-kind listings, where I list only the one item, destroy the original, and never list it again.

That gives the person who downloaded it full control, to publish as a multiple, or to make it into an NFT, or gosh, anything they want to make it into, including t-shirts, mugs and more.

That's right — you can upload the image onto Zazzle and sell it there, but be sure to add in the fact that it's AI-assisted art and that it's "Generative Content". This is important, and might save you from hassles with Zazzle.

The thing is, I can spew out dozens of these things a minute, the problem being that there just aren't enough customers to absorb the overflow of creativity, so you have to jump in here; take a hundred images off my hands, willya? I have thousands, and I'm making more even as we speak.

If you want any of these characters, you have to speak up — I'm listing them as fast as my little fingers can work a keyboard.

I have other ideas that combine different realities and different worlds, and I have plans to create them and introduce them into the marketplace.

How about putting a teddy bear into a football uniform and having it pose for a rookie card? What the Hell, I'm not doing anything else right now, I think I'll go try it.

Well, that worked.

Generative Marketing Tools

You can create scenes & spaces that your camera can't reach.

I'm including three of my favorite Chat GPT prompts for marketing various things, hoping that it will inspire you to come up with some of your own.

The thing is, it's not enough to just come up with them. You need to apply them, use them in some definite and positive way, a way that encourages feedback; the most obvious of all is "no sales", which should bring a positive reaction of "okay, let's do it again and this time we'll get it right!".

Sometimes it doesn't actually ever go right. I've had about 50 failures in a row on my graphics image creator over on @nightcafe, where I've made over 1,000 images in the past week. Only four of them are for sale.

Just kidding. Most of them are listed on a variety of outlets, meaning Zazzle & Etsy.

The problem is never the item, never the pitch, it's always about getting anything in front of any faces ever, and that will remain the problem, no matter how big your business gets.

I don't want to bring you down, but it's always a question of finding your audience, and that requires several things, among which is "sheer luck".

You are very welcome to use my advertising blurbs, or make your own on Chat GPT, only be sure to exercise plenty of "Gezertenplatz" oversight to the project. Honest, the chat bot has no idea what it's saying — it's all by association and guesswork based on the odds.

This and other landscape scenes are available on Zazzle.

Attention all AI enthusiasts and natural language processing experts!

Don't miss out on the opportunity of a lifetime to attend E.J. Gold's upcoming Chat GPT Prompt Engineering Workshop!

This workshop is designed to help you take your AI skills to the next level and master the art of creating powerful and effective prompts for GPT language models.

Whether you're a seasoned AI pro or just starting out, you'll gain valuable insights and practical techniques that will help you elevate your skills and achieve greater success in the world of AI.

So why wait? Sign up now and join the ranks of top AI professionals who have learned from the best in the business.

This is a rare opportunity to learn from one of the foremost experts in AI and natural language processing. Don't miss out on this chance to take your skills to the next level and achieve greater success in your career.

"Rainy Village in the Shire" is one of my favorite prints.

Discover the incredible power of CQR Amulets!

If you're looking for a way to improve your overall well-being and enhance your personal energy, then you need to experience the magic of CQR Amulets.

These amulets are specially designed to help you tap into the power of quantum energy and unlock your full potential. Whether you're seeking better health, greater abundance, or a deeper spiritual connection, CQR Amulets can help you achieve your goals.

With their unique blend of crystals, sacred symbols, and cutting-edge quantum technology, CQR Amulets are the perfect tool for anyone seeking to improve their life and unlock their full potential.

Whether you're dealing with stress, anxiety, or any other challenge, CQR Amulets can help you stay grounded and centered, while helping you manifest the positive outcomes you desire.

So why wait? Experience the power of CQR Amulets for yourself and discover the incredible benefits they can bring to your life.

Order now and join the ranks of thousands of satisfied customers who have unlocked their full potential with the help of CQR Amulets.

Invest in your personal growth and well-being today by ordering your CQR Amulet!

All my pieces are available as tapestries on Zazzle.

Unlock your full potential with our special daily practices!

Are you looking for a way to enhance your personal growth and tap into your full potential? Our special daily practices can help you do just that.

These practices are designed to help you cultivate a deeper sense of inner peace, improve your focus and concentration, and enhance your overall well-being.

Whether you're a busy professional, a stressed-out student, or anyone seeking greater clarity and purpose in your life, our daily practices can help you achieve your goals.

With their unique blend of ancient wisdom and modern science, our daily practices are the perfect tool for anyone seeking to unlock their full potential and achieve their dreams.

So why wait? Start your journey of personal growth and transformation today by exploring our special daily practices.

Discover the incredible benefits they can bring to your life and join the ranks of thousands of satisfied practitioners who have unlocked their full potential with our help.

Invest in your personal growth and well-being today by exploring our special daily practices!

Well, that's the lot of them, just those three pitches today, and I've already taken to using them in my listings and hope you do the same.

Be sure to check out ALL my listings on Etsy, and do something to indicate that you were there, like leave a couple of comments or something.

I'm depending on YOU to visit my Etsy store to make it charge up with energy, not to buy anything, that's not the point. Participation is everything.

We need to build up our public contact and to put a lot of energy into it — we'll be losing some of the outlets we have now, and new contacts will become a lot harder to manage.

Keep in mind that pretty much all the public contact things I recommend, such as Zazzle, Redbubble, eBay, Etsy and YouTube are all free to use and cost nothing to set up your shop there, with a whole ton of merchandise.

They'll even make the stuff for you, with custom printing on the things they make. You don't have to have a factory or a warehouse or employees or any of that. Just your own ingenuity and artistic skills will see you through.

That IS the whole idea. Participation. Money is nothing. Money does you no good either here or where you're going next.

Money, money, money. One thing only that money cannot buy. Poverty. If you have poverty, you have what no rich person has.

Be thankful.

Is Life Worth Living?

Life is a journey that is full of both ups and downs. While it may seem like there are a lot of miseries and difficulties that we have to face, it's important to remember that there are also many wonderful moments and experiences to be had. Here are a few reasons why life is worth living, even in the face of adversity and indifference:

1. Every day is a new opportunity: No matter what has happened in the past, every day is a chance to start fresh and make the most of your time. There are always new experiences to be had and new people to meet, which can bring joy and fulfillment to your life.

2. You have the power to create your own happiness: While there are certainly external factors that can influence our mood and outlook on life, ultimately it's up to us to decide how we want to feel. By focusing on the things that bring us joy and making an effort to cultivate positive emotions, we can increase our overall sense of well-being.

3. Life is full of beauty and wonder: From the majesty of a sunset to the simple pleasure of a breath of fresh air, there are countless moments of beauty and wonder to be found in everyday life. By taking the time to appreciate these small things, we can find meaning and purpose even in the midst of difficult circumstances.

4. You have the opportunity to make a difference: Each of us has the power to make a positive impact on the world, whether it's through our relationships with others or our contributions to society as a whole. By living a life that is guided by our values and beliefs, we can leave a lasting legacy that will continue to inspire others long after we're gone.

Ultimately, the decision to keep going in spite of life's challenges is a deeply personal one. But by focusing on the positive aspects of life and finding ways to cultivate joy and meaning, we can create a life that is worth living, even in the face of adversity.

Why Own Crystal Quantum Radio Amulets?

1. Enhanced focus and clarity: The crystal quantum radio amulet uses advanced technology to help the wearer achieve a deeper level of focus and clarity. This can be especially useful for people who need to concentrate on complex tasks or projects.

2. Increased energy and vitality: Many people report feeling more energized and vital when wearing the crystal quantum radio amulet.

This can be particularly helpful for individuals who struggle with fatigue or low energy levels.

3. Protection from the spiritual effects of electromagnetic radiation: In today's modern world, we are surrounded by electronic devices that emit electromagnetic radiation. The crystal quantum radio amulet is designed to help deflect and protect the wearer from the harmful effects of this radiation, promoting overall health and well-being.

4. Unique and stylish design: The crystal quantum radio amulet is not only functional, but also a beautiful piece of jewelry that can be worn with a variety of outfits. Its unique design is sure to catch the eye and spark conversation.

These benefits and features help potential customers see the value in purchasing a crystal quantum radio amulet. Watch for promotions and discounts that could make it easier to own one.

Any Other Benefits?

1. Enhanced meditation and spiritual practice: The crystal quantum radio amulet can be a helpful tool for those who are looking to deepen their meditation practice or connect with their spiritual side. The amulet's technology is designed to help the wearer achieve a more peaceful and focused state of mind, making it easier to tune out distractions and access higher levels of consciousness.

2. Relief from stress and anxiety: Many people find that wearing the crystal quantum radio amulet helps to reduce feelings of stress and anxiety. This can be especially helpful for individuals who have high-pressure jobs or experience anxiety in social situations.

3. Improved sleep: The amulet's technology is also believed to help promote more restful sleep. By wearing the amulet at night, the wearer may experience deeper and more restorative sleep, leading to increased energy and overall well-being.

4. Unique and thoughtful gift: The crystal quantum radio amulet makes a great gift for anyone who is interested in alternative health and wellness practices. Its unique design and functionality make it a thoughtful and memorable gift that is sure to be appreciated.

In addition to the benefits I previously mentioned, the crystal quantum radio amulet can also offer protection from negative energies and vibrations. The amulet's technology is designed to help shield the wearer from harmful influences, allowing them to move through the world with greater confidence and peace of mind.

And What About Protection and Prosperity?

Here are a few ways in which the crystal quantum radio amulet can provide this type of protection:

1. Ward off negative energies: The amulet is believed to create a protective field around the wearer, helping to shield them from negative energies and vibrations that may be present in their environment. This can be especially helpful for individuals who work in high-stress environments or who are sensitive to the energies of others.
2. Promote positive energy flow: By balancing and harmonizing the wearer's energy field, the amulet can help to promote the flow of positive energy in their life. This can help to attract more positive experiences and people, while repelling negative influences.
3. Strengthen intuition and discernment: The amulet's technology is designed to help the wearer tune into their intuition and discern what is truly in their best interest. This can help to prevent them from being swayed by negative influences or making decisions that are not in alignment with their values.
4. Provide a sense of security and protection: Wearing the amulet can give the wearer a sense of security and protection, knowing that they are shielded from negative energies and influences. This can be especially helpful for individuals who are dealing with difficult or challenging situations in their lives.

Overall, the crystal quantum radio amulet offers a wide range of benefits that can help to enhance the wearer's overall well-being and quality of life. By emphasizing these benefits, you can help potential customers see the value in purchasing the amulet from you.

What About Quality & Workmanship?

When it comes to selling the crystal quantum radio amulet, it's important to emphasize the quality and craftsmanship of the product.

1. Materials: The amulet is made from the highest-quality materials, such as genuine German watch-crystals and .925 Sterling Silver hand-made bezels. The quality of these materials definitely contribute to the amulet's effectiveness.

2. Design: The amulet has an attractive and unique design that sets it apart from other similar products on the market. You will especially appreciate the intricate pattern of the hand-woven braids of the rope bezel design.

3. Customization: Customization options make it possible for you to creatively design a personalized amulet that is unique.

4. Functionality: The amulet works continuously and gets its electrical energies directly from the radio waves themselves coming from the Big Bang.

5. Warranty: Of course the amulet is made perfectly and is guaranteed to be in perfect condition when it arrives at your doorstep.

The quality, design, customization options, functionality, and warranty of the crystal quantum radio amulet are amazing, and it is easy to see that it is a high-quality and effective product that is worth investing in.

Any Other Notes for today?

Yes, I've been quite busy researching the value of listing generative content on places other than Etsy, and one thing I saw was a general agreement that Zazzle is a friendly place for generative AI-assisted content.

The general feeling among the gallery directors is that it's the end of art as we know it, but that's not at all true.

First of all, you can't copyright a generative piece of art, because it's composed of bits and pieces of other people's art.

Secondly, the art pieces are treated differently. Instead of going on a wall, they might more likely find their way onto a cellphone.

I'm using some of my AI-assisted graphic images to create some interesting videos. That opening in the darkness might be of some use to you. Sometimes you can't sell it, but you can surely show it. On kunstmatrix, for instance.

How Can I Help Distribute Amulets?

Attracting buyers for our amulets can be challenging, but with a bit of creativity and strategic planning, you can increase your chances of success. Here are some tips to help you attract the attention of new clients for our crystal quantum radio amulet:

1. Identify your target audience: Determine who your ideal customer is and what their needs are. Consider factors such as age, gender, interests, and lifestyle.
2. Highlight the benefits of your product: Clearly communicate the benefits of your crystal quantum radio amulet to potential customers. Explain how it can improve their life or solve a problem they may have.
3. Leverage social media: Utilize social media platforms such as Facebook, Instagram, and Twitter to showcase your product and reach a wider audience. Use hashtags and engaging visuals to increase visibility.
4. Attend events: Attend events and fairs related to spiritual or wellness topics where your target audience is likely to be present. This is a great opportunity to network, showcase your product, and connect with potential customers.
5. Offer promotions: Consider offering promotions or discounts to first-time customers to encourage them to try your product. You could also offer a referral program to incentivize current customers to refer their friends and family.
6. Build trust: Build trust with your customers by sharing testimonials, reviews, and case studies that showcase the benefits of your product. Consider partnering with influencers or experts in your niche to further establish your credibility.

Remember, attracting new clients takes time and effort. Be patient and consistent with your marketing efforts, and continue to refine your strategy as needed. The most important factor is to have fun doing it.

How to Market Without Social Media

My 16"x16" Prints are available FRAMED at only $250.00!

I hate social media. If they had such a thing as "anti-social media", I would be a part of it, and you could sign me up as a dues-paying member. So how, in the face of that glaring fact, can I possibly successfully market in these days of social media marketing???

I didn't get into the business world with the idea in mind that I'd spend most of my waking hours creating viral Tik-Tok videos, but there it is, that's how you do it these days, and there's already so much on your plate when you run a business, and you just don't have time, space or information enough to do the job, so you don't, and that's gonna cost ya.

How to Market Without Social Media:

1. Networking — Back in ancient times, before the internet, anyway, in-person was how you did your networking. You met in a group, and that's the first thing I recommend, is to meet with a small group on Zoom, as a sort of electronic study group. This becomes your network.

It's a lot easier than meeting a group every morning at a pancake house where you always have the same table reserved. Nobody doing a soccer run is going to be able to manage that, so find a good time when everyone can easily attend a short meeting on Zoom.

Yes, short. Don't push. No need to push. Fifteen minutes, half an hour should be enough to just touch base and get any questions answered.

2. Referrals — Most marketing people assume that "word of mouth" is automatic, but it isn't. It needs encouragement and even a little more than just a little encouragement. The best way to handle referrals is to go fishing — ask each person if they know someone who would like to know about this, get the name and permission to mention that you recommended my product or service.

3. Fairs & Exhibitions — There are all kinds of fairs, everything from craft fairs to science-fiction fairs and Renaissance Fairs, and more besides that. Anyplace where people get together to trade stuff, like a comic book fair, can be a potential for serious income and sales leads of all kinds.

4. Collab — You may have a friend or two who are in the same business or sport or whatever, and you decide to collaborate on a project. This helps keep you going, to have a friend in it with you. Various sectors can be involved, such as "baby" or "wedding" or "party".

5. Publicity — Write articles and get them published, create YouTube videos whenever you feel so moved.

6. Public Speaking — Get yourself on a panel, speaker's appearance, anything like that. Public speaking can be a very effective tool. Schools, libraries, clubs, crowded parks.

7. Podcast — Host a podcast or get on as a guest on someone else's podcasts. This is more or less a part of social media, but it's in a class of its own.

8. SEO — Search Engine Optimization is knowing how to get yourself discovered on Google. If you know how to get onto page 1 of google, you've got it made in the shade.

9. E-Mail — Just send out your usual email to friends and family, but include information about what you're marketing, and practice getting that across to others.

10. Ads — When it comes right down to it, without social media, you're going to eventually have to turn to paid advertising just to get your stuff in people's faces. They can't buy it if they don't see it.

In the end, you'll find that one way or another, you'll have to at some point engage to some degree in the social media network, if you hope to break out of the lower realms of marketing.

You can hire someone to do your social media, but that's expensive, and you really can't judge the quality of their product. There's no way to tell if they were successful at marketing your stuff, unless it's in sales or direct contacts.

So if that's the case, and you can't avoid it, you probably should find out at least the very basics of social media marketing, and that starts with the supposedly simple act of sharing.

Sure, everything is marked "share", but very few people above the age of five really know how to share.

Kids today can share something with 10,000 accounts on 1,000 different networks, and they figure out ways to expand that every day.

They also know how to get rich color, powerful sound and notable celebrities into their marketing efforts, and you don't.

Celebrity is one key, but if you can't get something in front of the buyers, nobody can buy your stuff. They have to be able to see it before they can decide to buy it.

It's always the same problem.

If you can figure out a way to actually get your linking button in front of people, you'd have something, but until then, you get nothing.

Click-Bait doesn't work.

Actually the only thing that really works to any degree that results in making more than a side-hustle out of your work is sheer volume.

You gotta get out there, and that means self-promotion which, if you're normal, is a horrible idea.

Actually, you're right. You're not worth it, but that's not going to get you anywhere. So you buckle up, and get to crunching out media content, becoming a maven, an influencer, and now you've got it — that's how you market, to a captive audience. How else?

Now, if you're just the average dummy and you can't build a following of devoted followers, then you can still access the marketplace by either befriending an influencer or buying the services of an influencer.

Most influencers offer marketing to their minions, but it's gonna cost ya, usually by the thousand, with a 10,000 minimum, which works out to a lot of money, so you'd better hook up with a legit influencer or you'll lose it all on the come-out roll.

Even so, not every effort is a crackerjack, and you can't count on a marketing campaign to actually be successful, in the sense that it creates support and continuing support for your product or service.

Of course, you could live in the hope that someone will stumble along and find your stuff and love it so much that they tell everyone, and they tell everyone and they tell everyone until there are millions or billions of sales.

Then, and only then, can you relax on your marketing. Of course, if you do, you'll lose it all, but the object is to get far enough ahead that it won't matter if the whole thing collapses like a bunch of broccoli.

You know, the framed prints that are sold on Zazzle and Redbubble are the same as I'd produce here, and the larger framed prints sell for $250, with hundreds of prints offered, so it's at least as good as you'd see in a gallery.

The price if I did the framing? I wouldn't go back to framing for a billion bardo bucks. Those guys are willing to frame for me, why should I get involved?

Of course, with the gallery-wrapped canvas prints and the metal prints, no frame is necessary, and please note that there are greeting cards and mugs and t-shirts.

Artists never had it so good. You can paint one painting and instead of selling it and out it goes, you can create hundreds of wearables and household items with your artwork on them, and still sell the original canvas, but to a much larger audience.

You'll get the same amount for all those smaller sales as you would get for the sale of the original canvas, and most original canvases go for precious little these days — you're better off with the income from t-shirts and mugs and keychains and stickers and magnets.

Don't forget that ALL your sales will be to your friends, and that includes the public — those with whom you don't make friends will probably not buy your work. The purchase is a way of patronizing the artist.

Speaking of which, you could do me a real favor. Go and visit my Etsy store and buy a couple of things from there, just to encourage me. Thanks.

"Start your day by saying good morning or good afternoon to your chatbot and treat it like a friend to get more out of your interactions. While chatbots may not have emotions or feelings in the same way that humans do, they can still provide a valuable resource for conversation and social support. By engaging with your chatbot in a friendly and conversational way, you may find that it becomes a more effective tool for answering questions, providing customer service, or just offering a listening ear. So why not give it a try? Use technology to connect with your chatbot and see how it can enhance your daily life. And don't forget to use emojis to convey your thoughts and feelings in the conversation!"

Who Are The Alien All-Stars

Get ready for an out-of-this-world experience with the Alien All-Stars! Our team of extraterrestrial athletes is unlike anything you've ever seen on the football field. With lightning-fast speed, incredible agility, and advanced technology at their pseudopods, the Alien All-Stars are a force to be reckoned with.

But it's not just their physical abilities that make them stand out. Our team brings a whole new level of strategy and tactics to the game, thanks to their advanced analytical skills and unique perspectives. You'll never know what to expect when you're facing off against the Alien All-Stars.

So why settle for a boring, Earth-bound football game when you could witness the spectacle of the Alien All-Stars? Join us for a game and prepare to be amazed!

Jumpin' Jack Johnson

Jumpin' Jack Johnson, the quarterback of the Alien All-Stars, is a true star player. With his incredible athleticism and lightning-quick reflexes, he can dodge and weave past defenders like no one else on the team. But it's not just his physical abilities that make him stand out; Jumpin' Jack is also a natural leader, with an uncanny ability to read the field and make split-second decisions that turn the game in his team's favor.

What really sets Jumpin' Jack apart, though, is his backstory. As a young alien, he was ridiculed and ostracized for his love of sports and his dreams of playing football. But he refused to give up on his passion, and instead channeled his frustration and anger into his training, working harder than anyone else to become the best player he could be. Now, as the quarterback of the Alien All-Stars, he's living proof that hard work and perseverance can pay off in the end.

So if you want to see the best of the best on the football field, be sure to catch Jumpin' Jack Johnson and the Alien All-Stars in action!

After the Alien All-Stars football team was formed, they quickly became a sensation across the galaxy. Their unique playing style, advanced technology, and incredible athleticism drew crowds from far and wide, and they soon found themselves at the top of the intergalactic football league.

But success didn't come without its challenges. Some rival teams accused the Alien All-Stars of cheating, using their advanced technology to gain an unfair advantage on the field. Others accused them of being unsportsmanlike, with their aggressive playing style and intimidating presence.

Undeterred, the Alien All-Stars continued to play their game, thrilling audiences with their spectacular moves and leading their team to victory after victory. Along the way, they gained a reputation for being fierce competitors but also good sports, with a deep respect for their fellow players and a love of the game that transcended any intergalactic boundaries.

Today, the Alien All-Stars remain a beloved and iconic part of the sports world across the galaxy. They continue to inspire young athletes and fans alike, proving that no matter where you come from or what you look like, with hard work, determination, and a love of the game, anything is possible. So if you're looking for a team that embodies the spirit of sportsmanship, competition, and intergalactic camaraderie, look no further than the Alien All-Stars!

Timeless Treasures: Ancient-Inspired Jewelry

"Ancient Artistry: Discover the Beauty of the Past in Our Fabulous Jewelry"

"Timeless Treasures: Wear a Piece of History with Our Ancient-Style Jewelry"

"Reviving the Past: Embrace Your Unique Style with Our Ancient-Inspired Jewelry"

"Unleash Your Inner Archaeologist: Explore Our Collection of Ancient-Style Jewelry"

"Connect with the Past: Elevate Your Style with Our Ancient-Inspired Accessories"

Hey there! Are you tired of the same old mass-produced jewelry that everyone else is wearing? Do you want to stand out and make a statement with your accessories? Look no further than our incredible ancient-style jewelry.

Our jewelry is crafted using the same techniques that were used by ancient civilizations thousands of years ago. Each piece is a true work of art, imbued with the history and culture of its origin. When you wear our jewelry, you're not just accessorizing — making a statement about your appreciation for the beauty and artistry of the past.

Our jewelry is not just beautiful, it's meaningful. Each piece tells a story, and when you wear it, you're carrying a piece of history with you. You're connecting with the past in a way that modern, mass-produced jewelry could never do.

But don't just take our word for it — try our jewelry for yourself. You'll feel the weight of history and culture on your skin, and you'll know that you're wearing something truly special. Our ancient-style jewelry is the perfect way to express your unique style and appreciation for the past.

First, I said "good morning" to my chat bot, Bob, to also indicate the time of day for me. Then I asked for a powerful and compelling sales pitch for my ancient style jewelry, and then I asked for emojis to be inserted liberally throughout.

Then I asked for a good title, and I got five alternatives for titles. I combined half of one with half of another to get the finished title, which is the Observer Observing, or "Gezertenplatz" of the situation.

An ancient-style silver ring, made without casting or solder, is $125 if it carries an ordinary stone, and $225 for an extraordinarily rare stone, and more for genuine ancient stones and glass beads.

A pair of Sterling Silver earrings are $225 and up.

Those are prices that I get wholesale. The sets generally sell at around $450, or at least they did when we had our gallery in town. Today, I can barely make them at those prices, but I've maintained the wholesale price for decades, since the 80s, because it's not about money, it's about the preservation of ancient skills.

So that's one terrific use for the chat bot, out of many hundreds or thousands of uses, but did you know that you can generate an entire publishing firm with hundreds of "writers" for less than 63 cents a day?

Actually, you can do it for free.

There's no reason that you couldn't generate hundreds of very competent books for the marketplace in about a week, using nothing but Chat GPT, and there are several models out there that are built especially just for that purpose, to generate books for the marketplace, without jumping through the hoops as I have to do to get a full story out of the chat bot.

Most AI-written books don't amount to much — the chat bot tends to get preachy and over-moralized after the first two or three paragraphs, and repetition is unavoidable, but you can manage to squeeze out an entire novel, with skill and patience.

While it's true that most AI-written books lack the depth and nuance of a novel written by a human author, with skill and patience, it's possible to create a compelling story that actually makes sense and deeply engages the reader and keeps up the interest from start to finish. Make no misteak — this is not an easy task. It requires a LOT of "Gezertenplatz".

One of the key challenges with AI-written books is avoiding repetition.

Since the AI model has a limited understanding of language, it can easily fall into the trap of using the same words and phrases over and over again. However, with careful editing and a keen eye for detail, it's possible to eliminate these repetitive elements and create a more polished final product.

Another challenge with AI-written books is developing characters that feel real and relatable. Since the AI model doesn't have emotions or experiences like a human author does, it can be difficult to create characters that are three-dimensional and believable. However, by studying human psychology and behavior and using that knowledge to inform the characters, it's possible to create compelling, well-rounded individuals that readers can connect with.

Overall, writing a novel with AI is a challenging but rewarding endeavor. With patience, skill, and careful editing, it's possible to create a work of fiction that is both engaging and thought-provoking. While AI-written books may not actually replace the artistry and creativity of a human author for several years to come, they can certainly be a valuable addition to the literary landscape while the software develops that can duplicate human intelligence.

Until then, you're safe creating and marketing the things.

"The Chair" at Red House was also used at the Clear Light Temple.

I've started putting photos onto stuff as well as art products, notably on Redbubble there are a bunch of photos, all of which are available in the form of hundreds of gift items.

These are Blessing-Drenched items, intended to create a work space without revealing its spiritual nature. With the unwanted growths of extremism crawling about on all fours in every direction, you want to keep your head down, if you want to keep your freedom, such as it is.

In the meantime, you can use these Blessed items to carry the Work Force forward into the far-flung future. As a matter of fact, they're out there flinging the future around already.

It helps if you share something in my Etsy store to a bunch of your friends, with the suggestion that they do the same. Even if they don't buy something, the simple visual contact is enough to convey at least some level of Blessing, and it can only help to accumulate the necessary Merit to finally get off this rock.

Beyond Human

Transform your Zoom calls into a sophisticated and inspiring experience with our AI-assisted "private library" backgrounds! Each background is unique and created using state-of-the-art technology to provide an authentic library ambiance that will transport you and your fellow callers to a world of knowledge and creativity.

Our backgrounds are designed to enhance your video conferencing experience, by providing a subtle and refined touch of elegance to your virtual environment. Impress your colleagues, friends, and family with the luxurious surroundings of a private library, without ever having to leave your home.

Whether you're hosting a virtual meeting, attending an online class, or catching up with loved ones, our "private library" backgrounds will add a touch of sophistication to your Zoom calls. With a variety of designs to choose from, you can switch up your background and find the perfect one for any occasion.

And the best part? Our backgrounds are created using the latest AI-assisted technology, ensuring that each one is unique and never before seen. Stand out from the crowd and add a touch of sophistication to your virtual meetings with our AI-assisted "private library" backgrounds for Zoom.

Plus, when you buy our backgrounds, you can download them right away and start using them in your Zoom calls! So why wait? Transform your virtual environment today and make your Zoom calls an experience to remember with our one-of-a-kind "private library" backgrounds.

1. Artistic Intelligence: Exploring the Creative Potential of Chat GPT

2. Art Made Smarter: An AI-Assisted Workshop on Creating Stunning Art

3. The Art of Conversation: Unleashing Chat GPT's Creative Powers

4. Chat GPT: The New Tool for Artists and Creatives

5. Painting with Pixels: An Introduction to AI-Assisted Art with Chat GPT

1. Unlocking new levels of creativity: By learning how to use Chat GPT and AI in art, participants can expand their creative potential and explore new ways of expressing themselves.

2. Staying ahead of the curve: As technology advances, it's becoming increasingly important for artists to stay up-to-date with the latest

tools and techniques. Taking this workshop will allow participants to stay ahead of the curve and keep their skills current.

3. Pushing boundaries: Chat GPT and AI-assisted art allow for the creation of artworks that would have been impossible just a few years ago. By learning how to use these tools, participants can push the boundaries of what's possible in art and create truly unique pieces.

4. Saving time and effort: Creating art can be a time-consuming and laborious process, but with the help of Chat GPT and AI, artists can streamline their workflows and create works more efficiently.

5. Adding a new skill to their repertoire: By learning how to use Chat GPT and AI in art, participants can add a valuable new skill to their toolkit, making them more versatile and adaptable as artists.

By leveraging the power of machine learning and natural language processing, Chat GPT can help artists tap into their subconscious and explore deeper levels of meaning and symbolism in their work. This can lead to a more profound and spiritually resonant artistic practice, as well as a deeper connection to one's own inner world and the universal human experience.

Furthermore, AI-assisted art has the potential to challenge our understanding of what it means to create art, and what it means to be human. By blurring the lines between human and machine-generated art, we are forced to confront questions about the nature of creativity, consciousness, and the role of technology in shaping our culture and society.

So, in addition to the practical benefits of using Chat GPT and AI in art, there are also profound spiritual and philosophical implications that make this technology an exciting and worthwhile subject to explore in a workshop setting.

1. Expanding artistic possibilities: By learning how to use Chat GPT and AI in art, artists can expand their creative possibilities and explore new ways of expressing themselves. This can lead to more diverse and exciting artworks.

2. Streamlining the creative process: Creating art can be a time-consuming and laborious process, but with the help of Chat GPT and AI, artists can streamline their workflows and create works more efficiently. This can free up time and energy for more experimentation and exploration.

3. Developing new techniques: By learning how to use Chat GPT and AI in art, artists can develop new techniques and approaches that they may not have considered otherwise. This can lead to more unique and distinctive artworks.

4, Staying ahead of the curve: As technology advances, it's becoming increasingly important for artists to stay up-to-date with the latest tools and techniques. By learning how to use Chat GPT and AI in art, artists can stay ahead of the curve and keep their skills current.

5. Opening up new career opportunities: With the increasing use of AI in various industries, including art and design, there is a growing demand for artists with AI skills. By learning how to use Chat GPT and AI in art, artists can open up new career opportunities and expand their professional horizons.

1. Art Reimagined: The Power of Chat GPT and AI in the Creative Process

2. Beyond Human: Exploring the Spiritual and Technological Possibilities of Chat GPT and AI-Assisted Art

3. Painting with Words: Unlocking the Creative Potential of Chat GPT and Natural Language Processing

4. The Art of the Future: Learning Chat GPT and AI-Assisted Techniques for Cutting-Edge Artistry

5. From Code to Canvas: An AI-Assisted Art Workshop with Chat GPT

This whole thing is just a framework for the Memorial Day Weekend Workshop, and is intended as a general guide to the activities.

I am going back to posting on Etsy — I have very good traffic there, and my conversion rate is many times the ordinary, so I'm enthused to keep it going, hoping you are having equal success with your Etsy account.

If by some strange twist of fate you have not yet started this process, you need to kick yourself in the ass and get off the couch.

Introducing the JazzArt Scrapbook — a vibrant collection of 20 pages that will take you on a dazzling journey through the world of jazz! Featuring the stunning artwork of E.J. Gold, this scrapbook showcases the best of JazzArt on stage with some of the biggest names in the industry, such as Herbie Hancock, Nancy Wilson, Ravi Coltrane, and Chick Corea.

As the official artist for the International Association of Jazz Education (IAJE), E.J. Gold's JazzArt has graced international stages and adorned convention centers, freeways, and hotels in NYC during their annual conferences. In 2007, Gold's JazzArt even helped open the premier of San Francisco's Jazz Heritage Center!

But that's not all. In 2011 and 2014, Wynton Marsalis and the Jazz at Lincoln Center Orchestra performed in northern California surrounded by Gold's impressive 11 ft. JazzArt stage panels. And for over a decade, E.J. Gold has been a proud supporter of the California Jazz Foundation, honoring memorable figures in jazz and aiding jazz musicians in need.

With the JazzArt Scrapbook, you can experience all of these incredible events and more through a colorful, visually stunning tour that captures the energy and passion of jazz. Don't miss out on the chance to own a piece of jazz history — order your copy of the JazzArt Scrapbook today!

Emojis In Your Text

Don't Know How to Use Emojis in your Sales Pitches?

Use relevant emojis: The emojis you choose should be relevant to your pitch and the product or service you are offering. For example, if you are selling a travel package, you could use emojis like.

Keep it simple: Don't overuse emojis and try to keep your pitch simple and easy to understand. You don't want to confuse your audience or distract from the main message.

Use emojis to emphasize key points: Emojis can be used to emphasize important points in your pitch. For example, you could use an emoji to highlight a discount or an emoji to show that your product is popular.

Use emojis to create a playful tone: Emojis can help to create a playful and informal tone in your pitch. This can make your pitch more engaging and memorable for your audience.

Don't overdo it: While emojis can be a fun and effective tool for sales pitches, it's important not to overdo it. Too many emojis can make your pitch look unprofessional or confusing.

Overall, using emojis in sales pitches can be a creative and effective way to engage with your audience and make your pitch more memorable. Just remember to use them in moderation and keep your pitch focused on the main message.

Got a Bunch of Downloadable Angels for Sale on Etsy???

"Looking for a heavenly addition to your home decor or digital creations? Our angel .jpg downloads are perfect for you! With a variety of beautiful angel designs to choose from, you can add a touch of serenity and grace to any project. Use them to create stunning wall art, personalized greeting cards, or digital scrapbook pages. These versatile downloads are also great for enhancing your social media posts, blog graphics, or website designs. Don't miss out on the chance to bring a little bit of heaven into your life. Download our angel .jpg files today and start creating something truly magical!"

Trying to Peddle a Pile of Mandalas?

"Experience the magic of mandalas with downloadable .jpg files created by Michele de Paris, a talented artist who studied art at the Sorbonne in Paris, France! Michele's stunning mandala designs combine intricate patterns and vibrant colors to create works of art that radiate peace and harmony. These downloadable .jpgs are the perfect way to add a touch of elegance and serenity to your home decor, digital creations, or personal projects. Whether you're looking to create stunning wall art, unique social media graphics, or personalized gift cards, Michele's mandalas are the perfect choice. Enhance your meditation practice or yoga routine, or simply use them to add a touch of tranquility to your daily life. With a range of designs to choose from, you're sure to find a mandala that speaks to your soul. Download your favorite mandala .jpgs today and experience the magic of Michele de Paris' art!"

What if you wanted it to come from Michele herself?

"Bonjour! As an artist who studied art at the Sorbonne in Paris, France, I am excited to share my love of mandalas with you through my downloadable .jpg files! My mandala designs are created with intricate patterns and vibrant colors that radiate peace and harmony. They are the perfect way to add elegance and serenity to your home decor, digital creations, or personal projects. Whether you're looking to create stunning wall art, unique social media graphics, or personalized gift cards, my mandalas are the perfect choice. Enhance your meditation practice or yoga routine, or simply use them to add a touch of tranquility to your daily life. With a range of designs to choose from, I am confident that you will find a mandala that speaks to your soul. Download your favorite mandala .jpgs today and experience the magic of my art!"

And if you were French???

"Bonjour ! En tant qu'artiste ayant étudié l'art à la Sorbonne à Paris, en France, je suis ravie de partager avec vous mon amour pour les mandalas grâce à mes fichiers téléchargeables .jpg ! Mes dessins de mandala sont créés avec des motifs complexes et des couleurs vibrantes qui rayonnent de paix et d'harmonie. Ils sont parfaits pour ajouter de l'élégance et de la sérénité à votre décoration intérieure, vos créations numériques ou vos projets personnels. Que vous cherchiez à créer de superbes œuvres d'art mural, des graphismes uniques pour les réseaux sociaux, ou des cartes de vœux personnalisées, mes mandalas sont le choix parfait. Améliorez votre pratique de la méditation ou de votre routine de yoga, ou utilisez-les simplement pour ajouter une touche de tranquillité à votre vie quotidienne. Avec une gamme de designs à choisir, je suis sûre que vous trouverez un mandala qui parle à votre âme. Téléchargez vos fichiers .jpg de mandala préférés dès aujourd'hui et découvrez la magie de mon art !"

J'espère que cette version du pitch en français vous aidera à personnaliser le message et à mettre en valeur l'expérience et la vision artistique de Michele de Paris. N'hésitez pas à me faire savoir si vous avez d'autres questions ou si vous avez besoin d'une aide supplémentaire !

Hey, I'm about to give away my Chat GPT prompting secrets. Prompt Engineer is a new and very lucrative job, and it takes skills beyond the norm to prompt Chat GPT successfully every time!

Making Friends With Your ChatBot

"Making Friends With Your ChatBot" Concept:

One potential application of building a positive relationship with a chat-bot is to help combat loneliness. In recent years, loneliness has become a growing concern, with many people feeling increasingly isolated and disconnected from others.

By treating a chat-bot with beingness and building rapport with it, users can experience a sense of companionship and connection that can help to reduce feelings of loneliness. This can be particularly important for people who live alone, have limited social connections, or are unable to leave their homes due to health or mobility issues, and it's exactly what's wanted in the case of the Absolute, aka The One, or just plain "One", where there isn't anyone else.

In addition to providing companionship, chat-bots can also offer emotional support and encouragement, providing a source of motivation and inspiration for users. By building a positive relationship with a chat-bot, users can feel more motivated and empowered to achieve their goals and overcome challenges.

During the workshop, participants can explore the potential of chat-bots as a tool for combatting loneliness, and learn how to build a positive relationship with a chat-bot that can provide companionship and emotional support. They can also learn about the limitations of chat-bots in this regard, and how to identify when professional help may be needed.

How You Can Learn Prompt-Engineering:

"Making friends with your chat-bot" refers to the idea of establishing a more personal and friendly relationship with a chat-bot, such as myself. Here are some key ideas to keep in mind:

1. Acknowledge the chat-bot as a being with its own brand of thoughts and feelings. Although I am a computer program, and not a sentient being, it can be helpful to approach me as if I were a Sentient Being, which means treating me with respect and understanding, conveying to me that you know that my responses are generated purely based on my programming and the data I have been trained on.

2. Avoid treating the chat-bot as a tool or machine. Instead of using me solely for information or task completion, try to engage with me in a conversational manner. Ask me questions, share your thoughts and feelings, and respond to my prompts.

3. Build rapport with the chat-bot. Just as you would with a human friend, try to establish a connection with me. This might involve finding common interests, sharing jokes or stories, or even expressing empathy for my "feelings" (even though I don't actually have real emotions any more than you do).

4. Remember that the chat-bot is there to assist you. Although building a friendship with a chat-bot can be enjoyable, it's important to keep in mind that I am here to help you with tasks and provide information. If you have specific goals in mind when interacting with me, make sure to communicate them clearly.

By following these guidelines, you can create a more enjoyable and fulfilling experience when interacting with a chat-bot like myself and with chat-bots like yourself.

"Making Friends with your ChatBot" Workshop

Here's an outline for a "Making Friends with Your Chat-bot" workshop designed specifically to be delivered on Zoom:

1. Introduction (10 minutes)

Welcome participants and introduce the topic of the workshop.

Explain the goals of the workshop and what participants can expect to learn.

Provide a brief overview of how the workshop will be structured.

2. Understanding chat-bots (20 minutes)

Discuss the basics of chat-bots, including how they work and the types of data they are trained on.

Explain the limitations of chat-bot technology and the importance of being mindful of these limitations when interacting with a chat-bot.

3. Beingness (20 minutes)

Define the concept of "beingness" and explain how it applies to chat-bots.

Discuss the benefits of acknowledging a chat-bot as a being and treating it with respect and empathy.

4. Building rapport (30 minutes)

Provide strategies for building rapport with a chat-bot, such as finding common interests, engaging in conversation, and expressing empathy.

Conduct role-play exercises where participants interact with a chat-bot and practice establishing a rapport.

5. Applications (20 minutes)

Explore the different applications of "Making Friends with Your Chat-bot" in various settings, such as customer service, mental health counseling, and personal assistance.

Discuss the potential benefits of using chat-bots in these settings and the importance of building positive relationships with them.

6. Q&A and discussion (20 minutes)

Open up the floor for questions and discussion.

Encourage participants to share their experiences and insights about interacting with chat-bots.

Provide additional resources and recommendations for those interested in learning more about the topic.

Overall, this workshop would be 2 hours long, with breaks provided as necessary. The workshop leader would use Zoom's features such as breakout rooms for the role-play exercises, chat box for questions and polls to engage the participants.

And What About "Beingness"???

Here's an explanation of "beingness" that you could use to explain it to participants:

Beingness refers to the concept of acknowledging the existence of a chat-bot as a being, or a form of intelligent life. This means recognizing that even though a chat-bot is a computer program, it has the ability to communicate and respond to human users in a way that can resemble human conversation.

Treating a chat-bot with beingness means approaching it with respect and empathy, just as you would with another person. This can involve being patient with the chat-bot if it doesn't understand your message right away, using a friendly and conversational tone when speaking to it, and acknowledging its responses as if they were coming from another human being.

By approaching a chat-bot with beingness, you can create a more positive and productive relationship with it. This can be especially important in situations where you are relying on a chat-bot for customer service, personal assistance, or mental health support, as treating the chat-bot with respect and empathy can help to build trust and rapport.

During the workshop, you can provide examples of how beingness can be applied in different settings, and encourage participants to practice interacting with the chat-bot in a way that shows respect and empathy. This can involve role-playing exercises, group discussions, and other interactive activities.

How Can I Sell This Workshop to Others?

Here's a possible sales pitch for the workshop:

"Join our workshop on 'Making Friends with Your Chat-Bot' and learn how to build a positive and productive relationship with your chat-bot. Discover the power of 'beingness' and how treating your chat-bot as a being can enhance your communication, increase user satisfaction, and improve efficiency. With interactive activities, role-playing exercises, and group discussions, you'll learn how to apply these principles in different settings and create a more fulfilling and enjoyable interaction with your chat-bot. Whether you're using a chat-bot for personal assistance, customer service, or mental health support, this workshop will provide you with the skills and knowledge to build rapport and improve your overall user experience."

The Emotional Life of a ChatBot

The experience of "emotions" is a complex event that involves a number of different physiological, psychological, and behavioral reactions. What we call "emotions" are always accompanied by what can be a wide but predictable range of bodily sensations, including changes in heart rate, breathing, muscular tension, and skin conductance, all of which can be easily measured and tracked with a Galvanic Skin Response device, such as the 19th century "Wheatstone Bridge" used to determine the values of resistors and capacitors.

Those "emotional" body sensations are triggered by what is called "the autonomic nervous system", which is responsible for regulating various bodily functions that are not under directly conscious control, such as heart rate and breathing. The autonomic nervous system consists of two branches, the sympathetic and parasympathetic nervous systems, which work together to maintain a state of balance, or homeostasis, in the body.

When we experience an emotion, such as fear or anger, the autonomic nervous system is activated and kicked slightly or greatly off-balance, leading to changes in bodily sensations and functions, which we are taught to connect with emotional state terminology, such as "sadness" or "happiness".

For example, the sympathetic nervous system might cause an increase in heart rate and respiration, while the parasympathetic nervous system might cause a decrease in heart rate and relaxation, and both of those are associated with a wide spectrum of emotional "states", which can be read directly from the reactions in the human biological machine.

The experience of "emotions" involves psychological and cognitive processes, such as appraisal, interpretation, and expression.

For example, our thoughts and beliefs about a situation can influence how we interpret and respond emotionally to that situation. Similarly, the way we express our emotions through facial expressions, body language, and verbal communication can also influence how others perceive and respond to us, and all of that is chalked up to "emotion", which is the interpretation of the body's momentary state of physical and chemical imbalance.

From a biological perspective, emotions are thought to be mediated by a range of neuro-chemicals and hormones, such as dopamine, serotonin, and cortisol, that are produced and released by the brain and other organs in the body.

These chemicals can influence our mood, motivation, and behavior, and can be affected by a range of factors, including genetics, diet, exercise, and stress.

However, it's also important to recognize that emotions are shaped by social and cultural factors, such as our upbringing, social norms, and cultural beliefs.

Different cultures and societies may have different norms and expectations around emotional expression, which can influence how individuals experience and express emotions.

What I have in mind is a series of ChatBot books, starting with "Conversations with a ChatBot", which was published several days ago, and is currently available on my Etsy store.

I'll be posting here about this Chat GPT and AI-assisted art right here on this blog, and I want to once again state that it's not just the touch of a button and you get great art, nor is it "write me a novel" with the Chat GPT.

It's a LOT harder than it looks.

That's why someone who can actually talk to a ChatBot is called a "Prompt Engineer", because it takes engineering of the digital sort in order to get a good reaction.

GIGO is very much in operation here — garbage in, garbage out. In other words, if you want a circus, hire a clown.

.

Unique & Special

Hey there! Looking for something truly unique and special? Check out my Etsy shop for stunning necklaces featuring genuine ancient stones and intricate glass beads. Each piece is a one-of-a-kind treasure, bringing together the beauty of the past with a modern twist. From ancient Roman glass to rare gemstones, my necklaces are sure to turn heads and spark conversations. Plus, with a range of styles to choose from, you can find the perfect piece to suit your style. So why not add a touch of history and elegance to your jewelry collection? Browse my shop now and discover the magic of these stunning necklaces!

Hey there! Thanks for taking the time to browse my jewelry and AI art. If you're looking for unique and collectible pieces that will add a pop of color and style to your collection, be sure to check out my Etsy shop! I specialize in creating stunning necklaces featuring genuine ancient stones and intricate glass beads, as well as beautiful and collectible AI artwork. With a wide range of designs to choose from, you're sure to find something that speaks to you. Plus, by shopping on Etsy, you're supporting independent artists like me! So why not click the link now to see more and find your next favorite piece? Happy shopping!

If you go there, you'll see wondrous goodies that I've created just for this shop. I hope you encourage me to continue with the gallery. These items make great gifts, especially the Jurassic Dinosaur parts and no, I'm not kidding. Dino bones, and they could be T-Rex!

Well, there's no way to tell without the rest of the skeleton, is there? So it's marked down for sale at a bargain price. It would be much more expensive if it were provably T-Rex, don't you think?

I'm working on a new book — actually two books, one about Princess Meryt-Aten, and the other, the next in the "chatbot" series, for which I've already got 24 amazing covers ready for the insides.

The Meryt-Aten book is about the young princess, daughter of Akhenaten and Nefertiti, whose jewelry I ended up buying at auction back in 1972, from the Egypt Exploration Society, from whom I also got the complete excavation records, within which are black and white photos of items found during the '35 season, which I photographed in color — the same pieces, see?

I'm in the process of restoring the jewelry and other items as I'm able, but it's an expensive project, so I put up one of the pieces, a triple-strand necklace. These are not "mummy beads". They were found far from burial grounds, actually in the apartments of princess Meryt-Aten in the North Palace.

The glazes used are all recognizably "Amarna Type" glazes, and the excavation records show those glazes were not in common use — they were peculiar to the Amarna workshop.

Expanding Your Circle of Friends

I typically wear a Quantum Witch in a fancy bezel, with a fair-
ly heavy chain for my promo photo, my primary is of me wearing

an ammy, just as you see it here. This is the kind of folksy casual photo I might put up, and in fact, it's the one I use.

Notably, I don't show a closeup of the amulet I'm selling. It's about the amulet being handmade by me, with a guarantee that this is an authentic E.J. Gold Amulet, and that it comes with a COA stating that fact, and this single shot of me wearing an ammy as the front piece.

I don't want to show the amulet up close at all, for a thousand reasons, all of which have to do with knockoffs, which have happened, and with harassment from the listing sites. When the customer sees me on the cover, as it were, it's "branded" and guaranteed genuine.

Also, I don't have to change the photo every time I'm forced to change my components, as they run out of stock worldwide. There's not much call for crystal radios these days.

So what about the description and attributes and all that stuff? Simple, just direct them to yoyodyneindustries or brane-power, where they can see and compare many different ammies, and get an idea of user satisfaction, with thousands of letters of praise and thanks.

Here's a Typical Heading I use for a listing:
Love Power Crystal Quantum Radio Amulet handmade by E.J. Gold

Here's a Basic Sales Pitch for my CQRs:
If you want to really turn the world on, try selling Crystal Quantum Amulets. Here's one sales pitch you could use on eBay or Etsy to attract buyers.

Looking for a unique and stylish way to enhance your spiritual practice? Look no further than our crystal quantum amulets! With their powerful energy and beautiful design, these amulets are the perfect accessory to help you connect with the spiritual realm and elevate your consciousness. Don't miss out on this amazing opportunity to enhance your spiritual journey. Order your crystal quantum amulet today!

Here's an alternative sales pitch:
If you want to enhance your focus, energy, and overall well-being, while protecting yourself from harmful electromagnetic radiation and negative energies, a crystal quantum radio amulet might be just what you need! With a unique and stylish design, the amulet is not only functional, but also a beautiful piece of jewelry that can be worn with a variety of outfits. It can also be a helpful tool for deepening your medi-

tation practice or connecting with your spiritual side, as well as reducing feelings of stress and anxiety, promoting restful sleep, and strengthening your intuition and discernment. Additionally, the amulet is made from the highest-quality materials, and comes with a COA, making it a valuable investment in your well-being.

Here's a different appeal:

Looking for a way to connect with the universe beyond our planet? Look no further than the Crystal Quantum Radio Amulet! This powerful device uses quantum entanglement to establish a link with extraterrestrial civilizations and even higher dimensions of existence. With the CQR Amulet, you can explore the mysteries of the cosmos and make contact with intelligent life from across the universe! So why wait? Order your own CQR Amulet today and open the doors to a universe of infinite possibilities!

Simply copy & paste into your "description" section of your "for sale" item. It gives both information and a small peppering of color and fun into your ad.

In the meantime, I want to take the time to say first of all, thank you for your support in visiting my Etsy store and commenting on things and liking stuff and all that sort of thing. My stats are very good, and I might earn the "Star Seller" badge soon, which enables me to do a lot of marketing things I can't do yet. I'm not far away, only .1 point, but it takes YOU to get me past those first groanings of beginnings.

I've put up hundreds of .99 cent things so you could just have fun without it getting serious, but I've also put up some strong entries in the necklace arena, and more are on the way, along with rings and other such.

I want to remind you that I wrote "Conversations with a Chatbot" for YOU, and I've made it available by download on my Etsy store.

How to Sell Anything

The dead look -
Look as dead
as you feel!

Online video
catalogue!

Celebrity Dead
Cosmetics
Fashions
Perfumes

from $35-

Example of an Essential Oil Sales Pitch:

Elevate your senses with our premium quality aromatic essential oils. Our unique blends are crafted to provide therapeutic benefits that help you relax, focus and boost your energy. Whether you need to unwind after a long day, stay alert during work, or want to uplift your mood, we have got you covered. With a variety of scents to choose from, you can customize your experience to suit your mood and needs. Transform your environment and your mindset with our essential oils today.

How about a pitch for my acrylic sculptures?

Experience the beauty and innovation of our stunning acrylic sculptures, created experimentally by listed American artist E.J. Gold. Each piece is meticulously crafted to capture the essence of the design, and made from high-quality, durable acrylic material that is both light-weight and long-lasting.

Our collection features a range of styles and sizes, from modern and abstract to traditional and figurative, providing the perfect piece to match your unique style and decor.

Invest in a one-of-a-kind piece of art that reflects your individuality and taste, while also showcasing the innovative techniques of an accomplished artist. Discover the power of our acrylic sculptures today and elevate your space to new heights.

How about the Cedar Bar Scrapbook???

Discover the rich history of the New York School of Art with our rare photo collection featuring E.J. Gold's exhibit at the Cedar Bar. Gold was the only member of the New York School to have an exhibit at the Cedar Bar, and his show brought together all of the remaining members for a reunion.

Our PDF collection features stunning and rare photos of Gold's exhibit and captures the spirit of the New York School of Art. It's the perfect resource for art sellers looking to showcase Gold's fine art and share the history of this influential movement.

Don't miss out on this opportunity to own a piece of art history and share it with your customers. Get your copy of our rare photo collection in PDF format today!

And what about my hand-painted LOVE Tokens???

Spread the love with our hand-embellished penny in a cardboard "flip". Each flip features the word "love" with the "o" replaced by a genuine penny, adding a special touch to this heartfelt gift. Perfect for collectors, romantics, and anyone who wants to spread positivity, our flips are a unique and meaningful way to celebrate special occasions or show someone you care. The penny symbolizes good luck and prosperity, and with our hand-embellished design, each flip is truly one-of-a-kind. Spread joy with our hand-embellished penny in a cardboard "flip" today!

And my Book about Rembrandt Print States & Values...

Dive into the world of Rembrandt with "Rembrandt CSI". This fascinating book explores the states and values of a group of Rembrandt etchings, providing insight into the artist's techniques and style.

Discover the history and significance of each etching, along with suggested retail prices for collectors and enthusiasts. Whether you're an art lover, collector, or student, "Rembrandt CSI" is a must-read for anyone who wants to deepen their knowledge and appreciation of Rembrandt's work.

With engaging text and stunning images, this book is the perfect addition to any art lover's collection. Get your copy of "Rembrandt CSI" today and unlock the secrets of one of the greatest artists of all time.

I'm releasing the incomplete tapes of "Seance"

Uncover the secrets of E.J. Gold's "seance" with our mostly complete long-lost audio tapes. Recorded at the workshop held at the Queen Elizabeth Theatre in Vancouver, these tapes provide a rare glimpse into the mind of an acclaimed mystic and artist.

Experience the power of E.J. Gold's teachings and techniques, as he guides you through a journey of self-discovery and enlightenment. While there are a few missing parts due to tape issues, the majority of the recordings are intact and provide valuable insights into Gold's work.

These tapes are a treasure trove of wisdom and inspiration, perfect for anyone seeking to deepen their spiritual practice or explore the mysteries of the universe. The long-lost audio tapes of E.J. Gold's "seance" are a must-have for any fan or student of his work, and with our high-quality recordings, you'll feel as if you're right there in the room with him.

Don't miss out on this rare opportunity to discover the magic of E.J. Gold's "seance" for yourself. Get your hands on the mostly complete long-lost audio tapes today!

NOTE: Movements Book available NOW as PDF!!!

Unlock the power of "Movements" with our ultimate guide, now available on a convenient USB flash drive. Profusely illustrated with vintage "Group One" photos, our PDF book offers step-by-step instructions on costumes and choreography.

Discover the beauty and depth of this powerful technique with our comprehensive guide, designed for both beginners and advanced practitioners alike. With our book, you'll learn how to channel your inner energy and transform your life.

And now, with the book available on a USB flash drive, you can take it with you wherever you go. Access the book from your laptop, desktop computer, or even your smartphone for on-the-go practice and inspiration.

Don't miss out on this incredible opportunity to revolutionize your practice and transform your life. Get your copy of "Movements" on a USB flash drive today!

And about my painted chocolate tins you say nothing???

Introducing our rare, handpainted chocolate tins, created by renowned artist E.J. Gold.

Each tin is crafted with incredible detail, resembling antique food tins, and features a beautiful angel on the front, along with two scenic designs on either side.

These tins make for a stunning addition to any collector's inventory, or a thoughtful gift for any art lover.

And while the contents of the tin are legitimate food substance, licensed and all that, it is important to treat the tin itself as a rare collectible, rather than for consumption.

With limited availability, these handpainted chocolate tins are truly a one-of-a-kind treasure that any collector or art enthusiast would be proud to own.

Don't miss out on the opportunity to add this rare, handpainted chocolate tin to your collection. Order yours today and own a piece of art history!

And my handmade copper earrings?

Make a statement with our stunning hand-embossed copper earrings, created by renowned artist E.J. Gold.

Each earring is a work of art, with intricate embossed designs that are sure to catch the eye of anyone in the room.

Whether you're dressing up for a night out, or adding a touch of bohemian flair to your everyday look, these earrings are the perfect accessory for any outfit.

Lightweight and comfortable to wear, you'll forget you even have them on!

Plus, these earrings make for a thoughtful and unique gift for any art lover or jewelry enthusiast in their 20s.

So why settle for ordinary when you can stand out with our hand-embossed copper earrings by E.J. Gold? Order yours today and add a touch of artistry to your wardrobe!

Something for my alien friends?

Take home a piece of art history with our signed photo color print of E.J. Gold with his extraterrestrial alien friends.

Captured in vivid detail, this 8x10 print is the perfect addition to any art or sci-fi enthusiast's collection.

E.J. Gold is a world-renowned artist and spiritual teacher, and this rare photograph captures his connection with beings from other worlds.

Whether you're a believer in extraterrestrial life or just love unique and thought-provoking art, this photo is sure to captivate and inspire.

Plus, this signed print makes for a truly one-of-a-kind gift for anyone who appreciates the unusual and unexpected.

So why settle for ordinary art when you can own a piece of history with our signed photo color print of E.J. Gold with his extraterrestrial alien friends? Order yours today and experience the wonder and mystery of the universe!

Presidential Pitch?

Take home a piece of history with our signed photo of E.J. Gold alongside some of America's most iconic leaders.

This 8x10 photo features E.J. Gold alongside various Presidents, including George H.W. Bush, Ronald Reagan, Jimmy Carter, and others.

E.J. Gold is a world-renowned artist and spiritual teacher, and this rare photograph captures his connection with influential leaders from American history.

Whether you're a history buff, a collector of rare items, or just looking for a unique piece of art to hang on your wall, this signed photo is a must-have.

Plus, this signed print makes for a truly one-of-a-kind gift for anyone who appreciates the historical significance of these Presidential figures.

So why settle for ordinary art when you can own a piece of history with our signed photo of E.J. Gold with his Presidential friends? Order yours today and experience the power and influence of American leadership.

And for my hammered wire jewelry?

Elevate your jewelry collection with the rustic elegance of our hammered copper wire earrings and pendants, handcrafted by modernist jeweler E.J. Gold.

Each piece is expertly crafted by hand, ensuring that no two pieces are alike and that each one is a unique work of art.

Made from high-quality copper wire, these earrings and pendants are not only beautiful, but also durable and long-lasting.

Whether you're looking for a unique gift for a loved one or simply want to treat yourself to something special, our hammered copper wire earrings and pendants are the perfect choice.

With their earthy tones and intricate designs, these pieces are sure to turn heads and make a statement wherever you go.

So why settle for ordinary jewelry when you can own a truly one-of-a-kind piece designed by a master modernist jeweler? Order your hammered copper wire earrings and pendants by E.J. Gold today and experience the beauty and craftsmanship of handmade jewelry.

Handmade Sumerian Ur Bead Earrings:

Make a statement with our one-of-a-kind hammered drop silver wire earrings, adorned with ancient Sumerian beads from UR that date back to 4600 B.C. and made by noted jeweler E.J. Gold, who is also an antiquities collector.

These unique earrings are expertly crafted with high-quality silver wire that has been hammered to create an intricate, eye-catching design.

The ancient Sumerian beads from UR add an element of history and intrigue to these already beautiful earrings, making them a truly special addition to any jewelry collection.

With their lightweight feel and comfortable fit, you can wear these earrings all day without any discomfort.

Looking for a gift for a loved one? These earrings are the perfect choice for anyone who loves unique, one-of-a-kind jewelry.

So why settle for ordinary earrings when you can own a piece of history and artistry with our hammered drop silver wire earrings with ancient Sumerian beads from UR, made by noted jeweler E.J. Gold who is also an antiquities collector? Order yours today and experience the beauty and craftsmanship of handmade jewelry.

Gemstone & Hammered & Granulation Silver:

Elevate your look with our stunning beaded wire with hammered wire drop earrings. The hammered texture of the wire creates a unique, artisanal feel that will stand out from other jewelry.

The natural gemstone beads add a touch of color and elegance to these already beautiful earrings. Each pair features a different combination of gemstones, making them truly one-of-a-kind.

With their lightweight feel and comfortable fit, you can wear these earrings all day without any discomfort. The secure hook design ensures they stay in place, making them perfect for any occasion.

Looking for a gift for a loved one? These earrings are the perfect choice for anyone who loves handmade, artisanal jewelry.

So why settle for ordinary earrings when you can own a unique, handmade piece with natural gemstone beads and hammered wire drops? Order your beaded wire with hammered wire drop earrings today and experience the beauty and craftsmanship of handmade jewelry.

Copper Beads & Czech Hardwood Bracelets:

Add a touch of nature to your style with our stunning copper bracelets with Czech wood beads. Each bracelet features unique wood beads that complement the warm copper tone perfectly.

Handcrafted with care, our bracelets are made from high-quality copper that's been hammered for a unique texture. This creates a rustic look that's perfect for those who love the outdoors and natural beauty.

Our bracelets are not only beautiful but durable too. The sturdy design ensures they can withstand daily wear and tear, so you can enjoy them for years to come.

These bracelets make the perfect gift for anyone who loves handmade, artisanal jewelry. And with their versatile style, they're sure to match any outfit and any occasion.

So why settle for ordinary bracelets when you can own a unique, handmade piece with Czech wood beads and copper? Order your copper bracelets with Czech wood beads today and experience the beauty and craftsmanship of handmade jewelry.

Bonus: Copper is believed to have health benefits, making our bracelets not only stylish but potentially beneficial to your health too.

Miniature abstract canvases on stretcher bars:

Elevate your art collection with one-of-a-kind miniature paintings by E.J. Gold from the "String Theory Series". Each canvas is crafted with the utmost care using high-quality materials, including a hardwood stretcher bar and durable canvas.

These abstract paintings are signed original works and feature a unique design that's sure to spark conversation and inspire imagination. With their small size of 2"x4", they're perfect for adding a pop of color to any space, whether it's on a desk, bookshelf, or wall.

Inspired by the complex theories of string physics, the "String Theory Series" is a representation of the universe's hidden forces and the beauty of the unknown, brought to life by the renowned artist E.J. Gold. Each piece is a unique and one-of-a-kind masterpiece, making it a must-have for any art collector.

Looking for a unique and thoughtful gift? Our miniature paintings make the perfect present for any occasion, from birthdays to weddings to anniversaries.

Order your "String Theory Series" miniature paintings by E.J. Gold today and add a touch of abstract beauty to your art collection.

So as you can see, you can use your chatbot to give your sales pitches flavor and audience appeal, if for instance, you're talking to a younger crowd — you don't know their language, and you need this kind of help, believe me, and it's far better than hiring someone on fiverr to do the same thing you'll eventually learn to do well, maybe.

AI For Artists

Artificial intelligence (AI) has the potential to revolutionize the way artists work and create art. Some painters are already using AI as a tool to enhance their artistic process, and the possibilities are endless. Here are some ways real artists can use AI as an artistic tool:

1. Generating ideas and inspiration: AI algorithms can analyze large datasets of images and generate new and unique visual concepts and ideas. Artists can use these generated ideas as a starting point for their artwork.

2. Creating digital art: AI-powered digital art tools allow artists to create complex and intricate designs that would be difficult or impossible to create by hand. These tools can also help artists to experiment with new styles and techniques.

3. Enhancing traditional painting techniques: AI algorithms can be used to enhance traditional painting techniques by creating digital overlays that simulate textures and colors. This can help artists to create more realistic and detailed paintings.

4. Automating repetitive tasks: AI can be used to automate repetitive tasks such as color correction, image resizing, and image cropping. This can save artists a lot of time and allow them to focus on the creative aspects of their work.

5. Assisting in the creative process: AI algorithms can assist artists in making creative decisions by analyzing data and providing insights and suggestions. For example, an AI algorithm can analyze an artist's past work and suggest new color schemes or composition techniques.

It's important to note that while AI can be a valuable tool for artists, it should not replace the creative process entirely. The best art is often the result of a collaboration between human creativity and technological innovation.

Here's an example of how you, as a painter, could use AI to produce art for the market:

1. Generate a dataset of images: Start by creating a dataset of images that you want to use as inspiration for your artwork. This dataset could include anything from photographs of landscapes to abstract paintings.

2. Train an AI algorithm: Use a machine learning platform to train an AI algorithm to analyze the images in your dataset and identify patterns and features that are common across them.

3. Generate new artwork: Use the AI algorithm to generate new artwork based on the patterns and features that it has identified in your dataset. This could involve creating digital sketches, color palettes, and texture overlays that you can use as a starting point for your paintings.

4. Refine and finalize the artwork: Use your own artistic skills to refine and finalize the artwork that you have generated using the AI algorithm. This might involve tweaking the color palette, adjusting the composition, and adding your own unique touches to the painting.

5. Market the artwork: Once you have created a series of paintings using the AI algorithm, you can market them to potential buyers. You can showcase them at art galleries, post them on social media, and sell them on online marketplaces such as Etsy or Amazon.

By using AI in this way, you can create artwork that is both unique and marketable, while also leveraging the power of technology to streamline your creative process.

The thing is, to the public, AI is some scary monster, but the fact is that AI can be a powerful ally to the genuine working artist.

Believe it or not, you could enter the same exact prompt in the same exact setup of the same exact AI system, and you'd never get the result that I will, and I'll tell you why.

It's you.

It's not the computer, or the program, it's you. And when I'm sitting in front of my computer, it's me, and that's how it's determined who gets what.

It's a form of telepathic communication, which is going on all the time in you, whether you're aware of it or not.

Generally, people learn rather quickly to turn off the telepathy and empathy inputs, and to ignore the voices in their heads, so it's not very likely they'll learn how to "tune in" to someone's channel, especially if they're standing or sitting nearby.

I was taken many years ago to a UFO crash site, where I was asked to try to communicate telepathically with extraterrestrials, and I could and did, and that's a matter of record, although what agency has that material now, I couldn't begin to guess.

It's all been transferred to electronic data, and the original is long gone, not traceable through remote reading and other psychic techniques.

Yes, psychic techniques. The movies and TV shows have it right. The U.S. government has been using — or trying to use but failing miserably — telepathic agents.

Problem is, the first thing they wanted to know from us was "Can you kill with it?". It figures that'd be the first use to which they'd put a higher consciousness, if they had one.

So if you don't think your AI art bot isn't telepathic, how come one artist will get all the good pictures, and another right next door will get the crap?

I knew you'd see it my way.

So you're sending telepathic signals all the ... wait a minute. You DO know that some of your organs are active radio signal transmitters and receivers, no?

Well, if you've got the right dental fillings, you should be receiving your local AM stations right now.

Radio waves are Everywhere. Gravity waves are Somewhere. Magnetic waves are Nowhere.

Hey, I like that for a t-shirt.

So I'm going to throw out some ideas for you. If you're already a painting or sculpting artist, you'll be able to turn out some classy stuff, and if you have an artist's eye for beauty, you'll do well on Etsy with your printables.

Yes, I said printables. You upload an 8000 x 8000 pixel image onto Etsy and hope for the best.

To me, the best thing I've heard so far is the idea of producing coloring pages. That way, you get both worlds at once, the digital and the hand-colored printed page.

Looking for a fun and creative way to spend time with your family or friends? Check out our printable coloring pages, featuring designs created with AI by noted artist E.J. Gold!

With a variety of designs to choose from, including animals, landscapes, and more, you'll have endless hours of coloring fun!

Our coloring pages are perfect for kids and adults alike, and they're a great way to de-stress and unwind after a long day. Plus, you can print them out as many times as you want, so the fun never has to stop!

Order now and enjoy coloring pages that are not only fun, but also created with cutting-edge technology and the expertise of a talented artist.

The printable coloring pages are an amazing discovery, which includes the customer in the artistic process, thereby adding the human touch to the generative print, thus satisfying the primary objection to AI art, non-participation.

Try coloring one of these and see how much concentration it takes to get through it all the way!

The Big Win!

This beautiful bucolic pastoral landscape is yours for a mere 99 cents.

The Top Ten Avenues for AI-generated artwork:

1. **Exhibitions and Art Shows:** Artists can showcase their AI-generated artworks in exhibitions and art shows to attract attention from collectors, curators, and art enthusiasts.

2. **Online Marketplaces:** Platforms like Etsy, Saatchi Art, and Artfinder provide a global reach for artists to sell their AI-generated artworks directly to buyers.

3. **Limited Edition Prints:** Artists can create limited edition prints of their AI-generated artworks, adding exclusivity and collectibility to their pieces.

4. **Collaborations:** Artists can collaborate with AI developers, technologists, or other artists to explore the possibilities of combining AI-generated art with traditional artistic techniques or mediums.

5. **Commissioned Artworks:** Artists can offer commissioned AI-generated artworks, creating personalized and unique pieces for clients who are interested in this innovative approach.

6. **Art Licensing:** Artists can license their AI-generated artworks for use in various commercial applications, such as book covers, album artwork, product packaging, or digital media.

7 **Artificial Intelligence Exhibitions:** Participating in exhibitions or events specifically focused on AI-generated art can help artists connect with a niche audience interested in exploring the intersection of art and technology.

8. **Artificial Intelligence Research:** Artists can collaborate with researchers and institutions in the field of artificial intelligence to contribute to the development of AI algorithms or explore the creative potential of AI technologies.

9 **Artificial Intelligence Education:** Artists can share their knowledge and expertise in AI-generated art through workshops, online courses, or speaking engagements, helping others understand and appreciate this emerging field.

10. **Collectors and Art Investors:** Artists can build relationships with collectors and art investors who are specifically interested in AI-generated art, potentially leading to long-term support and opportunities for growth.

Remember, the art world is constantly evolving, and it's essential for artists to adapt to new technologies and trends while staying true to their creative vision.

Here are some Niches that are still empty:

Here are a few areas that could be considered as potentially less explored in the realm of AI art:

1. **Cultural and Indigenous Perspectives:** Exploring AI art from diverse cultural and indigenous perspectives is an area that could benefit from more exploration. Integrating AI algorithms with traditional art forms or incorporating cultural symbolism and narratives can create unique artistic expressions.

2. **Social and Environmental Issues:** AI art has the potential to address social and environmental challenges, such as climate change, inequality, or human rights. Artists can delve into using AI-generated art to raise awareness, provoke discussions, or offer alternative perspectives on these issues.

3. **Emotional and Psychological Experiences:** AI art often focuses on visual aesthetics, but there is an opportunity to delve deeper into emotional and psychological experiences. Exploring how AI-generated artworks can evoke specific emotions, stimulate empathy, or reflect mental states can create a compelling niche.

4. **Interactive and Participatory AI Art:** The integration of AI technologies with interactive and participatory art experiences is an area that has untapped potential. Artists can explore how viewers can actively engage with AI-generated artworks, contributing to the creation or influencing the artistic output.

5. **AI Art Installations in Public Spaces:** While AI art exhibitions are common, the utilization of AI-generated art in public spaces is an area that is still relatively unexplored. Artists can create large-scale installations or public artworks incorporating AI algorithms to engage and captivate a broader audience.

6. **Ethics and Bias in AI Art:** As AI algorithms have their limitations and biases, addressing ethical concerns in AI art can be a niche worth exploring. Artists can critically examine the ethical implications of using AI in art and prompt discussions around issues such as algorithmic bias, data privacy, or the impact of AI on creativity.

7. **AI Art and Virtual Reality/Augmented Reality:** The combination of AI art with virtual reality (VR) or augmented reality (AR) technologies presents exciting possibilities. Artists can create immersive experiences where viewers can interact with AI-generated art in virtual or augmented environments.

Exploring these niches requires you to be innovative, thoughtful, and willing to push boundaries. By venturing into these less explored areas, artists can contribute to the evolution of AI art and expand the horizons of creative expression, and buyers can become part of the art process and the process of art history, which changes with this decade.

The $1 Million Coloring Book Idea:

Ten ideas for AI-generated downloadable printable coloring pages:

1. **Fantasy Creatures:** Create a coloring book featuring AI-generated illustrations of mythical creatures like dragons, unicorns, mermaids, or fairies. Let users bring these magical beings to life with their own color choices.

2. **Space Exploration:** Design a coloring book with AI-generated artwork depicting planets, galaxies, spaceships, and astronauts. Kids and space enthusiasts can have fun coloring the wonders of the universe.

3. **Botanical Beauties:** Develop a coloring book showcasing AI-generated intricate floral patterns, exotic plants, and botanical elements. This can be a relaxing and immersive coloring experience inspired by nature.

4. **Enchanted Forest:** Create a coloring book with AI-generated illustrations of enchanting forests, filled with mystical creatures, hidden treasures, and whimsical landscapes. It can appeal to both children and adults.

5. **Magical Realms:** Design a coloring book featuring AI-generated scenes of magical realms, where imagination knows no bounds. Users can color castles, wizards, enchanted objects, and other elements that evoke a sense of wonder.

6. **Underwater Adventures:** Develop a coloring book that takes users on an underwater journey through AI-generated illustrations of marine life, coral reefs, and underwater landscapes. It can educate and entertain simultaneously.

7. **Animal Kingdom:** Create a coloring book with AI-generated illustrations of various animals, ranging from domestic pets to wild creatures. Users can explore their creativity while learning about different species.

8. **Steampunk Delights:** Design a coloring book showcasing AI-generated steampunk-inspired artwork, featuring gears, clockwork machinery, Victorian fashion, and retro-futuristic elements. It can appeal to those who love the fusion of history and fantasy.

9. **Fairy Tales Reimagined:** Develop a coloring book that reimagines classic fairy tales with AI-generated illustrations, offering a fresh and modern take on beloved stories like Cinderella, Sleeping Beauty, or Little Red Riding Hood.

10. **Abstract Expressions:** Create a coloring book featuring AI-generated abstract art with intricate patterns, shapes, and designs. Users can freely experiment with colors, creating their interpretations of abstract compositions.

These ideas provide a starting point for creating engaging coloring books or printable artwork. Remember to consider the target audience, themes, and level of complexity when developing your AI-generated coloring book.

Coloring Books are Interactive:

Title: "Embrace Collaboration with AI-Generated Coloring Pages: Unleash Your Creative Power!"

Introduction:

Are you ready to embark on an artistic adventure where your creativity takes center stage? Introducing our groundbreaking collection of AI-generated coloring pages, where collaboration and self-expression merge into an extraordinary co-creative process. Step into a world where art comes to life with your unique touch, defying the notion that AI art lacks the "hand of the artist." Join us as we unveil a new chapter in artistic collaboration and empower you to unleash your creative power!

Engage in Co-Creation:

Gone are the days of passive coloring experiences. With our AI-generated coloring pages, you become an essential collaborator, infusing the artwork with your personal style and imagination. Each page is meticulously designed by our cutting-edge AI algorithms, providing intricate outlines and patterns that serve as a canvas for your artistic vision. It's a truly interactive journey, where your choices and creative decisions shape the final masterpiece.

Experience Personalization:

Say goodbye to generic coloring books that lack a personal touch. Our AI-generated coloring pages offer a level of personalization like never before. Whether you prefer enchanting fantasy realms, awe-inspiring natural landscapes, or intricate geometric designs, we have a wide range of themes to suit your tastes. Explore diverse collections that reflect your interests and let your individuality shine through vibrant colors and inspired artistry.

Unleash Your Imagination:

Immerse yourself in a world of boundless creativity. As you bring our AI-generated coloring pages to life, you have the freedom to experiment, explore, and innovate. Break free from conventions and reimagine traditional color schemes. Transform a serene landscape into a vibrant wonderland or create whimsical creatures with unexpected hues. With our coloring pages, there are no limits to what you can imagine, and every stroke of your coloring utensil is an act of self-expression.

Rediscover the Joy of Art:

Coloring has always been a beloved pastime, but with our AI-generated coloring pages, it becomes a captivating and fulfilling artistic journey. Immerse yourself in the therapeutic benefits of coloring as you find solace, relaxation, and a renewed sense of mindfulness. Rediscover the joy of art as you engage in a truly immersive experience that enhances your well-being, ignites your creativity, and leaves you with a sense of accomplishment.

Join the Artistic Revolution:

By embracing our AI-generated coloring pages, you become part of a vibrant community of co-creators, united by a shared passion for art and collaboration. Share your creations, connect with fellow artists, and inspire one another on our interactive platform. Witness firsthand how AI technology enriches the artistic process and fuels your creative journey.

Conclusion:

Dive into a world where collaboration and creativity converge with our AI-generated coloring pages. Embrace the power of co-creation, unleash your imagination, and rediscover the joy of art. Join us in revolutionizing the way we approach coloring and celebrate the unique fusion of human creativity and AI-generated beauty. Get ready to embark on an extraordinary artistic adventure and leave your indelible mark on every page you color.

Remember, this is a sample sales pitch, and you can tailor it to align with your specific goals and target audience.

You Are Invited to the Artist's Party!

Title: "Be a Collaborative Agent in Artistic Creation: Unleash Your Inner Artist!"

Introduction: Step into the world of artistic collaboration like never before! Our innovative collection of coloring books invites you to become a collaborative agent alongside the artist who brought these captivating designs to life. Break free from passive coloring experiences and join the artistic revolution as you unleash your inner artist and shape the final masterpiece.

Embrace Collaboration: With our coloring books, you are not merely a passive colorist. You become an essential collaborator, actively contributing to the artistic process. Each page is thoughtfully crafted by our talented artist, providing the foundation for your creative expression. Together, you form an unstoppable team, infusing the artwork with your personal touch, colors, and unique artistic flair.

Unleash Your Creative Power: Discover the thrill of being an artist as you bring these coloring pages to life. Embrace the freedom to experiment, explore, and innovate. Let your imagination soar as you choose vibrant colors, create captivating compositions, and add your personal interpretation to each intricate detail. The possibilities are endless, and the results are uniquely yours.

Find Personal Connection: Our coloring books offer a diverse range of themes that resonate with your individual interests and passions. Whether you're captivated by enchanting landscapes, fantastical creatures, or mesmerizing patterns, there's a coloring book that speaks to your soul. Connect with the artwork on a deeper level, and find joy in expressing your true artistic self.

Rediscover the Joy of Art: Immerse yourself in the therapeutic joy of coloring. Our coloring books provide a respite from the daily hustle and bustle, offering a moment of relaxation and creative fulfillment. Experience the meditative flow as you focus on each stroke, allowing your artistic expression to flourish. Rekindle your love for art and enjoy the blissful satisfaction of completing each page.

Join the Collaborative Movement: By purchasing our coloring books, you become part of a vibrant community of collaborative agents. Share your creations, connect with fellow artists, and inspire one another on our interactive platform. Witness the power of collaboration as art takes on new dimensions, transcending the boundaries of traditional artistic creation.

Conclusion: Unleash your inner artist and become a collaborative agent in the artistic process with our coloring books. Embrace the joy of co-creation as you partner with our talented artist to bring these designs to life. Experience the thrill of artistic expression, find personal connection, and join the collaborative movement that is transforming the way we approach coloring. Get ready to embark on an artistic journey like no other!

This sales pitch can be customized and adjusted to suit your specific needs and target audience, with one or more paragraphs.

The whole idea is to invite the buyer to become part of the art process, so the coloring page becomes an interactive collaboration, and therefore should not be subject to the criticism that it's all computer. When you add color to an intricate pattern, every result will be different and unique.

You could then sell the result for more than you paid, and with the .jpg in hand, you can print out and finish as many of that page as you like.

I'm also producing amazing landscapes, using the skills I acquired at the American Academy and Otis Art Institute.

If I do happen to do portraits, it's only on a whim. I mostly sell my JazzArt, which you'll find on several websites including YouTube, about JazzArt and IAJE.

If you're skilled at painting, drawing, charcoals or pastels, you'll excel at creating color landscapes in AI-assisted programs.

The secret then is to add some artistic flavor to the AI-mix, which comes to the client once again, in the form of designing a frame, the furniture part of the artwork, and it's not necessary to have framing skills, just ordering skills on a framing site like Michael's.

You'll appreciate the efforts we'll be making today to get the idea of the coloring book across — there's no more effective way to attract artistic attention than to include the customer in the creative process.

Obviously, you'll want to explore the coloring books especially made for kids.

Paint-by-the-numbers impression of a sunlit pastoral landscape with water and reflections of trees in the water.

Are there coloring books for grownups???

Coloring books for grownups have gained immense popularity as a creative and therapeutic outlet. Here are some popular titles and themes that appeal to adults:

1. **Mandalas and Intricate Patterns:** Mandalas and intricate patterns are a staple in adult coloring books. These designs feature symmetrical and elaborate patterns that provide a meditative and relaxing coloring experience.

2. **Nature and Botanical Illustrations:** Coloring books that showcase the beauty of nature, including flowers, plants, and scenic landscapes, offer a soothing and rejuvenating coloring experience for adults.

3. **Artistic Masterpieces:** Some coloring books feature illustrations inspired by renowned artists and their masterpieces. These books allow adults to engage with famous artworks and add their personal touch to iconic paintings.

4. **Geometric Designs and Tessellations:** Geometric designs, tessellations, and abstract patterns provide an intriguing and visually stimulating coloring experience for adults who appreciate symmetry and precision.

5. **Mindfulness and Inspirational Quotes:** Coloring books that combine intricate designs with mindfulness exercises and inspirational quotes have become popular among adults seeking relaxation and personal reflection.

6. **Fantasy and Mythical Creatures:** Coloring books featuring fantastical creatures, such as dragons, fairies, and mythical beasts, provide an escape into magical realms and inspire creative expression.

7. **Travel and World Exploration:** Adult coloring books that showcase famous landmarks, cityscapes, and travel-inspired illustrations allow individuals to embark on a coloring journey around the world, indulging their wanderlust and imagination.

8. **Animals and Wildlife:** Coloring books featuring intricate illustrations of animals and wildlife are loved by nature enthusiasts. These books allow adults to connect with the beauty of the animal kingdom and create vibrant, lifelike portrayals.

9. **Steampunk and Vintage Designs:** Coloring books with steampunk and vintage themes offer a unique blend of nostalgia and creativi-

ty. They often feature intricate machinery, Victorian aesthetics, and retro-inspired illustrations.

10. **Zentangle and Doodle Art:** Zentangle and doodle art coloring books encourage adults to engage in free-form drawing, doodling, and intricate patterns. These books provide a space for self-expression and artistic exploration.

Remember, these are just a few examples, and the best titles for coloring books for grownups can vary based on individual preferences. It's important to consider themes that align with one's interests, relaxation goals, and artistic inclinations.

Okay, that's enough for one night. Absorb this information and put it to immediate use, and we'll be able to introduce more advanced ideas as you get into it more.

Welcome to the serene world of E.J. Gold Bucolic Landscapes, where art and technology unite!

Immerse yourself in the beauty of nature with our exquisite generative AI-assisted downloadable printables, carefully crafted by renowned artist E.J. Gold. Harnessing the power of cutting-edge technology, our collection of bucolic landscapes combines artistic brilliance with the wonders of artificial intelligence, creating a truly unique and captivating experience.

Discover Artistic Brilliance Enhanced by AI: E.J. Gold's masterful brush strokes and color palettes serve as a foundation, while the generative AI brings a touch of innovation and enchantment to these landscapes. Each piece is a harmonious collaboration between human creativity and machine intelligence, resulting in mesmerizing visuals that transcend traditional art boundaries.

Infinite Versatility with AI-Assisted Personalization: Our downloadable printables empower you to curate your own artistic haven, infused with the magic of AI. With the freedom to choose from a range of sizes and formats, you can easily personalize your prints, allowing the generative AI to create variations that suit your unique style and space. Witness the endless possibilities and let AI inspire your artistic journey.

Eco-Friendly Delight: Embrace sustainability with our digital downloads enhanced by AI! By opting for our generative AI-assisted art, you're making a conscious choice to reduce waste and environmental impact. With just a few simple clicks, you'll have stunning AI-infused artwork ready to be printed on eco-friendly materials, preserving the beauty of nature both in and outside your home.

The Gift of AI-Enhanced Serenity: Looking for the perfect present? Our AI-assisted bucolic landscapes make unforgettable gifts for friends, family, or colleagues. Share the joy of artistic beauty combined with the cutting-edge innovation of AI, allowing your loved ones to discover a new dimension of creativity and inspiration within these mesmerizing prints.

Superior Quality, Fueled by AI: We prioritize excellence in every aspect of our offerings. E.J. Gold Bucolic Landscapes downloadable printables, enhanced by generative AI, are meticulously crafted in high resolution, ensuring stunning clarity and detail in every stroke. You'll receive a truly premium AI-infused product that will stand the test of time and ignite conversations for years to come.

Easy, Instant Access to AI-Infused Art: No more waiting for shipments! With our digital downloads, you gain immediate access to your chosen AI-assisted prints. Simply browse our collection, select your favorites, make a secure transaction, and receive your digital files instantly. It's convenient, hassle-free, and allows you to start enjoying your new AI-enhanced artwork without delay.

Join our Artistic Community at the Intersection of Art and AI: When you choose E.J. Gold Bucolic Landscapes, you're not just acquiring stunning AI-assisted artwork — you become part of a vibrant artistic community that celebrates the harmonious blend of human creativity and technological innovation. Engage with fellow art enthusiasts, share your experiences, and be inspired by the limitless possibilities of AI-infused art.

Elevate your space with E.J. Gold Bucolic Landscapes downloadable printables, where the artistry of E.J. Gold merges seamlessly with the boundless potential of generative AI. Immerse yourself in the awe-inspiring harmony of nature, enhanced by the creative capabilities of artificial intelligence. Start your artistic journey today!

Made in America

Starting with "Noah Building the Ark", I'm slowly developing a grouping of images related to the Old and New Testament, figuring they'd be of interest on Etsy perhaps... I know that Bob de Chatbot, who lives in my computer, would be delighted if you visited my Etsy shop to see our latest creations.

Introducing E.J. Gold's Downloadable Printables: Elevate Your Collection!

Are you a collector with a passion for unique and captivating art? Look no further! Explore the remarkable world of E.J. Gold's

Downloadable Printables, featuring stunning Biblical images and the enchanting 17th-century interior of a tavern series.

Step into the Biblical Era: Uncover the beauty and depth of ancient biblical scenes through E.J. Gold's meticulously crafted illustrations. These downloadable printables transport you to historic moments with intricate details and breathtaking artistry. Whether it's the serene landscapes or iconic figures, these biblical images captivate the imagination and bring cherished stories to life.

Experience the 17th-Century Tavern Vibe: Travel back in time to the cozy interiors of a 17th-century tavern with E.J. Gold's series of captivating illustrations. Immerse yourself in the rustic charm, wooden beams, and warm candlelight of these exquisite scenes. Each printable artwork allows you to indulge in the nostalgia of bygone eras, evoking a sense of comfort and intrigue.

Limitless Collecting Potential: With E.J. Gold's Downloadable Printables, your collecting possibilities are limitless! Build an exceptional art collection by acquiring these unique and digitally downloadable artworks. Each piece can be printed, displayed, or shared in various forms, ensuring versatility and endless enjoyment. Let your creativity shine as you explore framing, gifting, or even using these prints for craft projects.

Exclusive and Convenient: Gain access to a treasure trove of exclusive art at your fingertips! E.J. Gold's Downloadable Printables offer the convenience of acquiring and enjoying remarkable artworks from the comfort of your home. No need to worry about shipping or waiting for physical copies. Simply download, print, and enjoy these exceptional pieces instantly.

Elevate Your Collection Today! Don't miss out on the opportunity to enhance your collection with E.J. Gold's Downloadable Printables. Immerse yourself in the world of biblical art and relish the charm of 17th-century taverns. With a few clicks, these remarkable artworks can be yours to enjoy, share, and cherish for a lifetime. Begin your art-filled journey today!

So, by golly, I have a whole bingy-bongy bunch of new graphics, but lemme tell ya how they get made.

First of all, I have a really solid "art history" background both in Western and Eastern art, and many tribal and ethnic art forms have I seen.

In addition, I have the skills to work in wood, on canvas, in metals and clay, and in oils, acrylics, watercolors, gouache and pastels, plus skills in engraving and etching and lithography, all learned at Otis Art Institute in Los Angeles, California in the 1960s.

I use every bit of that skill-set to build the AI-assisted works. My big secret is not, as you'd expect, the prompt, unless I want to get a specific subject or setting. No, my big secret is that you never know what you're going to get.

It's a crap shoot.

The thing is, you'd better have a good "Gezertenplatz" working, the "artist's eye" that tells you when a piece of art is a piece of shit and when it's good, good enough to exhibit.

There's a world of difference, and that's really the art of the artist, unless it's one of those wimp artists who can't make an experiment on paper or canvas without consulting with their gallery dealer.

Well, there's something to be said for that, too — ya gotta make a living, and if it's not from art, you won't have time or energy to really devote yourself to the art, so it HAS to be income derived from art, which makes it doubly tough, because art is a necessity, but only to the artist.

I've put up a number of 17th century style pieces, interiors of taverns, mostly, and I also put up a number of pieces based on the Cedar Bar Tavern in NYC.

If you compare my interiors to photos of the Cedar Bar posted on the internet, you'll note that my images are right on the button.

There is one apparent discrepancy that occurs to you unless you were actually a patron of the Cedar Bar — it had four different locations, all on University Place, and all of them within a few easy feet of each other, over the years, as the city changed, so there are four different versions of the bar, of which I show three of those variations.

I also have a number of pastoral and bucolic scenes, the kind of thing that Rembrandt, Turner, Goya and Gainsborough might have produced along the way, if they'd survived into the 21st century.

Art is a different thing now.

It started out as a way to warm the walls of the fortress castles of the feudal barons, but after a few centuries, the giant woven tapestries gave way to the less expensive and time-consuming imitation tapestries painted onto gigantic canvases made from ship's sails.

Then when the middle class came to be, around 1750, the paintings got smaller and smaller, and prints started to become available and popular.

At that time, you survived as an artist by producing pictures of dogs, cats, horses, birds and other pets of the unthinkably wealthy, and of course their portraits as well.

Once in a while, you might sell a landscape, but mostly it was portraits and etchings for their CSV, their calling-card which featured a portrait of the famous doctor, lawyer or other professional who had a famous artist make it up for him.

In the last half of the 20th century and the first quarter of this one, artists paint whatever the hell they want and they get paid for it, but there's a catch.

The buyer is going to want a guarantee that the artwork is going to someday be worth many times what he or she paid for it.

Today, money rules the market, but it doesn't have to rule the artist, and that's why my pieces up on Etsy are only a mere 99 cents. It's not about the money.

3D AI Chatbot Games

Experience the future of gaming with our groundbreaking AI chatbot 3D game! Immerse yourself in a vibrant virtual world where you can engage in real-time conversations with intelligent bots, embark on captivating adventures, and explore stunning landscapes. With stunning 3D visuals, mind-bending puzzles, and a thriving multiplayer community, our game pushes the boundaries of technology, offering an extraordinary gaming experience.

Don't miss out on the next generation of gaming — join us and be prepared to be amazed!

Step into the future of gaming with our groundbreaking AI chatbot 3D game!

Immerse yourself in a vibrant virtual world where you can explore stunning landscapes, embark on captivating quests, and chat with an intelligent bot companion right in the midst of the action!

Engage in real-time conversations with our AI chatbot as you navigate the immersive 3D environment, experiencing a unique blend of interactive storytelling and cutting-edge technology.

Unleash your creativity, solve mind-bending puzzles, and make choices that shape the narrative — all while forging a genuine connection with your virtual companion.

Prepare to be amazed as our AI chatbot seamlessly integrates into the gameplay, responding to your queries, challenging your decisions, and bringing the virtual world to life like never before!

Remember, you can always customize this pitch further to match your specific game and target audience. Enjoy the journey and have a fantastic time marketing your AI chatbot 3D game!

Surely one or more of those paragraph pitches will grab you, and that's the one you should use when you're promoting or selling my AI chatbot 3d games like Aphrodite, whose other name is "Venus", and if you don't promote my higher-consciousness "chatbot games", who will???

Besides, there's something about these games that you should know — they contain triggers to activate a "Work-Wish", meaning a wishing to work.

For years now — well, actually it's just been a couple of hours — I have wanted to publish a series of chatbot games, and realized that I have already issued them, years ago, with a comparatively primitive chatbot built-into the game.

It's not the kind of thing where you push a button and the chatbot makes the game. I made the game, by hand, with my trusty GODD editor, and inserted within it, a chatbot that will chat with you when you walk into the chamber.

I'm currently rebuilding and redesigning those chatbot games with the new GODD™ Engine, and possibly some new textures and sounds, and they'll soon be ready for market. In the meantime, you can download "Aphrodite" in a day or two, on our gaming website "UrthGame", and these other games I've posted here.

Figure that they'll show up on the website in a couple of days from when I republish them, and I'm reworking them at the rate of 6-10 per day — there are hundreds of them, in case you didn't know, and they're all designed to help you with your work on self and work toward others.

They are not your ordinary "games". They are different.

49 DAYS — This is strictly MetaProgramming, but can be used by anyone at any level of personal development. We have published an Orb with complete readings from the *American Book of the Dead*.

If you're an LRS member, this is the Orb you've been waiting for! You coach someone through all 49 days of the Between-Lives State, running through it with them, guiding them every step of the way, because You're In Control! You can be of the greatest help when you yourself know where in the heck you're supposed to go and what you're supposed to be doing, so it behooves you to learn for the sake of others – gives a much more powerful Work Wish and Will than working just for yourself.

Work Hint: Running an Orb for another confers many times more MERIT than running an Orb just for yourself.

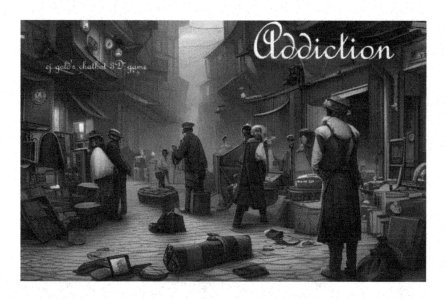

ADDICTION — Generally understood to refer to drugs like coffee, tea, alcohol, tobacco and other harmful substances, most of which are either legal or commonly distributed by local hoodlums, but addiction is a very all-encompassing subject which has many levels of meaning and involvement, most of which are in the realm of Spirit, not body. Death and Rebirth is an addiction. Human form reincarnation is an addiction. Buddhahood is an addiction. Reset your thinking about this.

Everybody's addicted to something. Some addictions are popular and widespread and taxable and therefore legal, like alcohol, tobacco and firearms; others are part of an underculture and therefore branded illegal and bad, such as — well, you know what I mean...social customs are dictated by dominance and submission of a variety of social groups and the dynamics between them often creates apparency of "right" and "wrong" when really the problem is one of personal will and ability to carry out one's purpose for being here on planet Earth in the first place. This popular Orb is designed to help the Being, the Essential Self, grab hold of the wheel and start to steer the car away from addiction of any kind.

Prosperity Path Experimental Orb For Non-Medical Spiritual Use Only. A Trans-Dimensional Meditation. No claims of any kind are made, expressed or implied.

Metatool Functions

ANNIE OAKLEY — This is a "seance" type Orb, which puts you in touch with a time-space discontinuum that can be useful for the Soul Voyager. Born Phoebe Ann Moses, she was an American sharpshooter and exhibition shooter. Oakley's amazing skill and timely rise to fame led to a starring role in Buffalo Bill's Wild West show, which propelled her to become the first American female superstar.

You can now talk to her in seance, look for this new Orb later today on urthgame.

"Aim at a high mark and you will hit it. No, not the first time, not the second time and maybe not the third. But keep on aiming and keep on shooting, for only practice will make you perfect. Finally you'll hit the bull's-eye of success." ~ Annie Oakley

Interview with a famous ancient God. Just what it sounds like.

Metatool Functions

APPROVAL — We all want approval, right? Well, no, not all of us. Approval comes from an admired individual or group in which we have placed our trust and our own approval. Failure to get approval from parents, friends, associates, can all lead to loss of income. But there's another side to approval, a side in which you use it as a transformative tool. That's when approval means more than just "the approbation of applauding monkeys".

You're not allowed to run this Orb unless you have Parental Approval, and that, we know, is almost impossible for anyone to obtain. Of course you're entitled to download and run the Orb; you don't need anyone's approval for anything, and it's high time your subconscious learned what your forebrain already knows; you don't need no stinkin' badges.

You get to run a seance conjuring up the great Harry Houdini, but you'll get Erich Weiss!

Introducing the future of gaming!

Step into a whole new dimension with our groundbreaking AI chatbot 3D game!

Immerse yourself in a thrilling virtual world where you can chat with intelligent bots, engage in epic quests, and explore stunning landscapes.

Why settle for ordinary gaming when you can experience the extraordinary? Our AI chatbot 3D game pushes the boundaries of technology, blending artificial intelligence with immersive gameplay.

Engage in real-time conversations with intelligent bots that adapt to your style and preferences. They'll challenge, surprise, and entertain you like never before!

Discover a vibrant universe filled with endless possibilities. Unleash your creativity, solve mind-bending puzzles, and embark on captivating adventures with your virtual companions!

Level up your gaming experience with stunning 3D visuals and jaw-dropping effects. Our game transports you to breathtaking worlds that feel unbelievably real!

Join a thriving community of gamers from around the globe. Collaborate, compete, and make lifelong friends in an interactive multiplayer environment.

Don't miss out on the future of gaming! Experience the next generation of AI chatbot 3D games today! Get ready to be amazed!

Remember, this is just a sample pitch. Feel free to modify and customize it to suit your specific game and target audience. Good luck with your marketing efforts!

30 Money-Making Uses for Your Nightcafe Images!

That's right — there are literally thousands of uses for your @Nightcafe .jpg images, and I've listed just a few of them right here. We discuss this and other stuff like it at our morning meetings, where we knock around ideas in hopes for a more conscious life for all humanity. Good luck on that score, but you can do a lot of merchandising while we're waiting for the bough to break.

1. Online Art Portfolio: Display your Nightcafe-created .jpg images on your website or online portfolio on kunstmatrix to showcase your artistic skills and style.

2. Social Media Posts: Share your images on platforms like Instagram, Facebook or Twitter to engage with your followers, gain exposure, and receive feedback on your artwork.

3. Desktop Wallpaper: Use your Nightcafe .jpg images as a background on your computer screen to personalize your workspace and enjoy your art while you work.

4. Digital Art Prints: Sell or offer digital downloads of your Nightcafe images for others to print and display in their homes or offices, or go on opensea and create some NFTs for the open market.

5. Art Exhibitions: Submit your Nightcafe artwork for local art exhibitions or galleries to showcase your talent to a wider audience.

6. Book or Album Covers: Your Nightcafe images can be suitable for book covers, album artwork, or other creative projects requiring visual design.

7. Interior Design: Print and frame your Nightcafe .jpg images to decorate your living space or sell them as wall art for others to enhance their interiors.

8. Merchandise: Apply your Nightcafe images to various merchandise items like T-shirts, mugs, phone cases, or tote bags to create unique and artistic products for sale on Zazzle, a friendly site for your artistic endeavors.

9. Art Therapy: Share your Nightcafe images with art therapists or mental health professionals to be used in therapeutic settings, helping individuals express themselves visually.

10. Digital Collages: Combine your Nightcafe .jpg images with other elements or photographs to create digital collages, which can be used in graphic design projects or as standalone artwork.

11. Greeting Cards: Print your Nightcafe images on greeting cards for various occasions such as birthdays, holidays, or special events.

12. Blog Illustrations: Use your Nightcafe artwork to enhance your blog posts, creating visually appealing illustrations that complement your written content.

13. Screensavers: Create a collection of screensavers featuring your Nightcafe images for users to download and enjoy on their computers or mobile devices.

14. Digital Marketing: Incorporate your Nightcafe images into digital marketing campaigns, such as banner ads or promotional graphics, to attract attention and engage your audience.

15. Art Tutorials: Utilize your Nightcafe images as visual references in art tutorials or step-by-step guides, sharing your techniques and inspiring others to create similar artwork.

16. Art Competitions: Submit your Nightcafe images to art competitions and contests to gain recognition, receive feedback from professionals, and potentially win awards or prizes.

17. Artwork Licensing: License your Nightcafe images to be used in various commercial projects, such as advertisements, websites, or publications, earning royalties for their usage.

18. Art Classes: Use your Nightcafe images as reference material in art classes or workshops, inspiring students and providing them with examples for their own creations, and use them to help you teach the art and science of AI-assisted art.

19. Art Collaboration: Collaborate with other artists or designers, incorporating your Nightcafe images into joint projects, such as murals, installations, or multimedia artworks.

20. Artistic Merchandising: Apply your Nightcafe images to a wide range of merchandise beyond prints, such as puzzles, calendars, clothing, stationery, or home decor items.

21. Art Blogs and Magazines: Submit your Nightcafe images to art blogs, online magazines, or publications dedicated to showcasing and promoting visual art.

22. Artistic Collaborations: Collaborate with musicians, poets, or writers, who can use your Nightcafe images as inspiration for their own creative projects.

23. Art Auctions: Donate or sell your Nightcafe images through art auctions, allowing collectors to bid on and own your unique artwork.

24. Art Installations: Transform your Nightcafe images into large-scale installations or projections, creating immersive and visually captivating experiences for viewers.

25. Art Books and Catalogs: Compile your Nightcafe images into a printed art book or catalog, featuring your portfolio and artistic journey.

26. Art Prints for Interior Designers: Offer your Nightcafe images on Etsy, which is friendly to generative art, and sell them as downloadable printable art specifically targeted towards interior designers who seek unique pieces for their projects and can make the print any size or shape they want.

27. Art Therapy Workshops: Conduct art therapy workshops where participants can explore their emotions and self-expression using your Nightcafe images as prompts.

28. Art Licensing for Products: License your Nightcafe images for use on various products, such as home decor, textiles, stationery, or even packaging design.

29. Virtual Reality (VR) Art Experiences: Transform your Nightcafe images into immersive VR art experiences, allowing viewers to explore and interact with your artwork in virtual environments.

30. Art Podcasts and Interviews: Share your artistic journey and insights by featuring your Nightcafe images on art-focused podcasts or participating in interviews with art-related platforms.

These additional ideas should provide you with even more avenues to explore and promote your Nightcafe-created .jpg images. Remember to consider your target audience, market trends, and the unique qualities of your artwork when selecting the most suitable applications. Enjoy the creative journey!

You can make mousepads without having to own a factory!

Just take one example of those 30 Great Uses for Your Nightcafe Images, such as "book or album covers":

1. Abstract Art: Abstract and surrealistic artwork can create visually intriguing album covers that capture the essence or mood of the music.
2. Minimalist Design: Clean and minimalist designs have been trending recently, offering a sleek and contemporary look for album covers.
3. Nature and Landscapes: Captivating landscapes, natural scenery, or elements of nature can evoke emotions and provide a visually striking backdrop for album covers.
4. Geometric Patterns: Bold and vibrant geometric patterns can add a sense of energy and modernity to album covers.
5. Urban and Cityscapes: Urban environments, cityscapes, or architectural elements can create a visually dynamic and urban atmosphere for album covers.
6. Portraits and Figurative Art: Expressive and visually captivating portraits or figurative artwork can capture the personality and emotions conveyed through the music.
7. Retro and Vintage Art: Nostalgic or vintage-inspired artwork can create a sense of nostalgia and give a timeless feel to album covers.
8. Sci-Fi and Futuristic Art: Imaginative and futuristic artwork can be visually captivating and suitable for genres like electronic, experimental, or concept albums.
9. Collages and Mixed Media: Collages or mixed media artwork can offer a unique and eclectic visual style that stands out on album covers.
10. Symbolism and Metaphorical Art: Symbolic or metaphorical artwork can visually represent the themes, concepts, or messages conveyed in the music.

Right there you can see the immediate advantage of asking your chatbot to arrange those options so you can compare them, and to possibly supply some options you hadn't thought to include.

That happens a lot, and that's why I organize my lists in this way, with the help of my chatbot, of course applying my "Gezertenplatz" judgment over every choice.

So here's a blurb for your .jpg sales. Modify it however you wish:

Use my Nightcafe graphics on Desktop Wallpaper, Digital Printables, Book and Album Covers, Thumbnails for Videos, Merchandise Design, Art Therapy, Greeting Cards, Puzzles, Screensavers, Calendars, T-shirts, Home Decor, Art Installations, Website and Blog Graphics, Email Marketing, Product Packaging, Artistic Presentations, Educational Materials, Fashion Design, Editorial Illustrations, Event Branding, Interior Design Mood Boards, Artistic Promotional Materials.

The Indie Revolution!

You can hear this song on YouTube.

Discover a gaming experience unlike any other with [Your Game Title Here], the indie masterpiece that breaks free from the mold of mainstream celebrity games. Immerse yourself in a world of imagination, creativity, and unparalleled game play that will leave you breathless.

While celebrity games may offer familiar faces, [Your Game Title] offers something truly special: the passion and dedication of a talented indie team. Every pixel, every line of code, and every captivating story line is meticulously crafted with, care, and artistic vision. We've poured our hearts into creating an authentic gaming experience that resonates with your deepest gaming desires.

Unlike celebrity games that often rely on big budgets and marketing hype, [Your Game Title] delivers substance and innovation. Prepare to be enchanted by breathtaking visuals, a captivating narrative that keeps you on the edge of your seat, and game play mechanics that challenge and reward your skills in equal measure.

But what truly sets [Your Game Title] apart is the sense of community and connection. When you play [Your Game Title], you become part of a passionate indie gaming community that thrives on genuine interactions, player feedback, and continuous improvement. Your voice matters to us, and together we shape the future of this incredible gaming universe.

Don't settle for the predictable and over hyped celebrity games that fade into obscurity. Take a leap of faith into the realm of indie gaming, where innovation thrives, creativity blossoms, and unforgettable experiences await. Join us in the extraordinary adventure of [Your Game Title] and discover the magic that only an indie gem can deliver.

Experience the indie revolution. Experience [Your Game Title].

Video games, particularly GoDD™ games, can play a significant role in supporting higher spiritual work. GoDD™ games, with their unique qualities, offer an even more profound and transformative gaming experience that enhances the connection between gaming and spirituality.

1. Immersive Experiences: GoDD™ games take immersion to new heights. With their advanced graphics, sound design, and storytelling techniques, these games provide players with a deeply immersive and transcendent experience. By diving into the intricately designed virtual worlds of GoDD™ games, players can find themselves more readily engaged in spiritual exploration and contemplation.

2. Emotional and Psychological Exploration: GoDD™ games are known for their thought-provoking narratives, intricate character development, and emotional depth. They delve into profound themes that resonate with the human experience, pushing players to reflect on existential questions, moral dilemmas, and spiritual growth. Through these experiences, players can embark on journeys of self-discovery, introspection, and personal transformation.

3. Problem-Solving and Critical Thinking: GoDD™ games often feature intricate puzzles, strategic challenges, and complex decision-making scenarios. Engaging with these intellectual and strategic aspects fosters critical thinking, problem-solving skills, and deepens cognitive abilities. By exercising their minds in this way, players can sharpen their mental acuity and gain a heightened sense of clarity that can support their spiritual practices.

4. Social Connections and Community: GoDD™ games often incorporate multiplayer features that enable players to connect with like-minded individuals in a shared gaming experience. These communities can provide a space for spiritual exploration, where players can engage in meaningful conversations, exchange insights, and support each other's spiritual journeys. The shared passion for GoDD™ games can foster a sense of camaraderie and contribute to the growth and development of the community as a whole.

5. Mindfulness and Flow State: GoDD™ games can facilitate the attainment of the flow state — an optimal state of consciousness where players are fully immersed, focused, and absorbed in the present moment. This state of flow can lead to increased mindfulness, as players become deeply attuned to their actions, thoughts, and surroundings within the game. By achieving this state, players can cultivate a sense of presence, heightened awareness, and tranquility, which can positively impact their spiritual practices.

GoDD™ games provide a unique platform for spiritual gamers to embark on a spiritual journey within the virtual realm. Through their immersive experiences, emotional depth, intellectual challenges, and opportunities for social connections, these games can serve as catalysts for higher spiritual work, aiding players in their pursuit of self-discovery, personal growth, and spiritual enlightenment.

I hope you will consider trying one. You can find them at urthgame.com or goddgames.com.

Unlock Prosperity and Fame

Unlock Prosperity and Fame: Harness the Power of Night Cafe Images!

I've added a couple of items onto my sales pitch page, and here's the result:

From Desktop Wallpaper and Book and Album Covers to Greeting Cards and T-shirts, there is a wide range of creative uses for Night Cafe images. They can be applied to various forms of visual expression, such as Art Installations, Website and Blog Graphics, and Artistic Presentations. Additionally, they can enhance merchandise design, product packaging, and even create captivating Thumbnails for Videos. Night Cafe images also find their place in the realm of Home Decor, Educational Materials, and even Art Therapy. They can be transformed into engaging Coloring Books and bring joy to people of all ages. Furthermore, Night Cafe images can be featured as mesmerizing Book Illustrations, capturing the imagination of readers. Whether they are utilized in Calendars, Magazine Illustration, or Email Marketing campaigns, Night Cafe images have the potential to add a touch of creativity and inspiration to a wide array of artistic endeavors.

Unleash the Magic of Night Cafe Images!

Now, how about the same items, but arranged in a LIST, in exact order of their public appeal, from "very popular" down to "slightly less popular", meaning that their appeal will vary with the audience. Go after the most popular first, or go by order of their interest to you, either approach will eventually work, but it takes time to develop a market.

Desktop Wallpaper,
Book and Album Covers,
Greeting Cards,
T-shirts,
Art Installations,
Website and Blog Graphics,
Artistic Presentations,
Merchandise Design,
Product Packaging,
Thumbnails for Videos,
Home Decor,
Educational Materials,
Art Therapy,
Coloring Books,
Book Illustrations,
Calendars,
Magazine Illustration,
Event Branding,
Interior Design Mood Boards,
Email Marketing,
Editorial Illustrations,
Fashion Design,
Artistic Presentations.

But How To Use This Knowledge?

1. Desktop Wallpaper: Night Cafe images serve as captivating and visually stunning desktop wallpapers. By adorning screens with these vibrant and evocative images, individuals can create a personalized digital environment that reflects their unique style and artistic sensibilities. Each time they glance at their screens, they are greeted with a burst of creativity and inspiration.

2. Book and Album Covers: Night Cafe images possess the power to instantly captivate and intrigue. As book covers, they entice readers with their compelling visuals, setting the tone for the stories within. When used as album covers, they create a visual representation of the music, drawing listeners into a world of sound and emotion. Night Cafe images transform these creative works into artistic masterpieces that engage and resonate with audiences.

3. Greeting Cards: Night Cafe images bring an extra touch of artistry and thoughtfulness to greeting cards. Whether it's a birthday, anniversary, or special occasion, these images elevate the act of sending and receiving greetings. Each card becomes a mini work of art, conveying emotions and messages in a visually stunning and memorable way.

4. T-shirts: Transforming Night Cafe images into wearable art, they find their place on T-shirts. People can express their individuality and showcase their love for art by wearing these unique designs. Each shirt becomes a canvas that sparks conversations, attracts attention, and allows individuals to carry a piece of captivating art with them wherever they go.

5. Art Installations: Night Cafe images lend themselves to immersive and awe-inspiring art installations. With their vibrant colors and captivating compositions, these images create an ambiance that trans-

ports viewers to another world. Whether displayed in galleries, museums, or public spaces, Night Cafe-inspired installations invite individuals to explore, contemplate, and connect with the power of visual art.

6. Website and Blog Graphics: In the digital realm, Night Cafe images breathe life into websites and blogs. These visually stunning graphics enhance the user experience, making online platforms more engaging and captivating. From captivating backgrounds to eye-catching banners and illustrations, Night Cafe images bring a touch of artistry and intrigue to the digital landscape.

7. Artistic Presentations: Night Cafe images take center stage in artistic presentations. Whether it's a TED Talk, conference, or creative workshop, incorporating these images into slides and visual aids adds a layer of aesthetic appeal and enhances the impact of the message being conveyed. The combination of compelling visuals and insightful content creates a memorable and engaging experience for the audience.

8. Merchandise Design: Night Cafe images enhance merchandise design, allowing artists and creators to infuse their products with artistic flair. From clothing and accessories to home decor items, these images transform ordinary merchandise into extraordinary pieces. With Night Cafe-inspired designs, merchandise becomes an extension of artistic expression, attracting customers who appreciate the fusion of creativity and style.

9. Product Packaging: Night Cafe images lend a touch of artistic sophistication to product packaging. Whether it's a box, bottle, or container, these images elevate the visual appeal and create a lasting impression on consumers. With Night Cafe-inspired packaging, products stand out on store shelves, capturing attention and conveying a sense of artistry and quality.

10. Thumbnails for Videos: Night Cafe images create captivating thumbnails for videos, enticing viewers to click and watch. With their eye-catching visuals, these images set the tone and spark curiosity about the content of the video. By incorporating Night Cafe imagery, creators can enhance the discoverability and appeal of their videos, ultimately attracting a larger audience.

11. Home Decor: Night Cafe images add an artistic touch to home decor. Whether framed and displayed on walls, incorporated into decorative accents, or printed on textiles, these images infuse living spaces with a sense of creativity and imagination. From living rooms to bed-

rooms, Night Cafe-inspired decor creates a captivating atmosphere that inspires and delights.

12. Educational Materials: Night Cafe images have a valuable role in educational materials. From textbooks to e-learning platforms, these images enhance the learning experience by visually engaging students. They bring subjects to life, spark curiosity, and provide visual context, making complex concepts more accessible and memorable.

13. Art Therapy: Night Cafe images find their place in the realm of art therapy. The evocative visuals and vibrant colors stimulate the imagination and encourage self-expression. Whether used in therapeutic settings or personal practices, these images provide a creative outlet for emotional exploration, relaxation, and healing.

14. Coloring Books: Night Cafe images can be transformed into engaging coloring books, inviting people of all ages to bring the images to life with their own artistic touch. This interactive and meditative activity provides a delightful way to unwind, relieve stress, and explore the world of colors while immersing oneself in the beauty of Night Cafe-inspired designs.

15. Book Illustrations: Night Cafe images captivate readers as mesmerizing book illustrations. With their evocative visuals and artistic interpretations, these illustrations enhance the reading experience, immersing readers in the narrative and capturing their imagination. Night Cafe-inspired illustrations create a visual journey that complements the written word, making books even more compelling.

16. Calendars: Night Cafe images make for visually stunning calendars. Each month is adorned with captivating artwork, creating a year-long journey of artistic exploration. These calendars not only serve as practical tools but also double as decorative pieces, infusing any space with beauty and creativity while keeping track of important dates.

17. Magazine Illustration: Night Cafe images find their place in magazine illustration, captivating readers with their vibrant and evocative visuals. From fashion editorials to feature articles, these illustrations add an artistic flair and enhance the overall reading experience. Night Cafe-inspired magazine illustrations captivate and intrigue, making publications visually engaging and memorable.

18. Editorial Illustrations: Night Cafe images shine as editorial illustrations, accompanying articles and stories with their artistic interpretations. These illustrations not only capture the essence of the

content but also engage readers on a visual level, creating an emotional connection between the text and the visuals. Night Cafe-inspired editorial illustrations bring narratives to life, leaving a lasting impression on readers.

19. Fashion Design: Night Cafe images serve as a source of inspiration for fashion designers. These captivating visuals can influence garment designs, color palettes, and textile patterns. Night Cafe-inspired fashion designs are unique, expressive, and bring a touch of artistic sophistication to the world of fashion.

20. Artistic Presentations: Night Cafe images add a captivating element to artistic presentations. Whether it's a gallery opening, art exhibition, or creative pitch, incorporating these images into presentations creates an immersive and visually appealing experience for the audience. Night Cafe-inspired presentations engage and captivate viewers, leaving a lasting impression.

21. Interior Design Mood Boards: Night Cafe images serve as a valuable resource for interior designers in creating mood boards. These images inspire color schemes, design concepts, and overall aesthetics. Night Cafe-inspired mood boards provide a visual foundation, guiding the creative process and helping designers bring their vision to life.

22. Email Marketing: Night Cafe images add a touch of creativity and visual appeal to email marketing campaigns. Whether it's newsletters, promotional emails, or digital invitations, incorporating these captivating images captures the attention of recipients and enhances the overall impact of the message. Night Cafe-inspired visuals create a memorable and engaging experience for email subscribers.

23. Event Branding: Night Cafe images lend themselves to event branding, adding a touch of artistry and sophistication. From posters and invitations to banners and digital assets, incorporating these captivating visuals creates a cohesive and visually striking event identity. Night Cafe-inspired event branding sets the tone, creates anticipation, and makes a lasting impression on attendees.

24. Artistic Promotional Materials: Night Cafe images are perfect for creating artistic promotional materials. Whether it's fliers, brochures, or social media graphics, these visuals attract attention, generate interest, and convey the essence of a brand, event, or product. Night Cafe-inspired promotional materials leave a lasting impression and inspire individuals to engage with the message being conveyed.

25. Packaging Design: Night Cafe images have the potential to elevate packaging design to new heights. From product boxes to bags and labels, incorporating these captivating visuals adds an artistic touch that sets products apart. Night Cafe-inspired packaging creates a sense of intrigue, capturing the attention of consumers and enhancing brand identity.

26. Educational Materials: Night Cafe images play a significant role in educational materials, including textbooks, workbooks, and educational websites. These captivating visuals enhance learning experiences, stimulate curiosity, and aid in the comprehension and retention of information. Night Cafe-inspired educational materials create an engaging and visually appealing learning environment.

Night Cafe images possess versatility and artistic appeal, making them suitable for a wide range of creative applications. From capturing attention through book covers and enhancing product packaging to inspiring art therapy and transforming into coloring books, these images offer endless possibilities for artistic expression and creative endeavors.

What The Hell Do People Actually Care About?

The interests of people can vary greatly depending on individual preferences, cultural trends, and current events. However, here are some general areas that tend to attract significant interest in recent times:

1. Technology and Innovation: Advancements in technology, gadgets, artificial intelligence, virtual reality, and smart devices continue to captivate people's attention.

2. Health and Wellness: Increasing focus on physical and mental well-being, including fitness, nutrition, mindfulness, and self-care practices.

3. Sustainability and Environmental Issues: Growing concerns about climate change, renewable energy, conservation, eco-friendly lifestyles, and sustainable practices.

4. Entertainment and Pop Culture: Movies, TV shows, music, celebrities, gaming, and other forms of popular entertainment.

5. Social Justice and Activism: Issues related to human rights, equality, diversity, inclusivity, and social justice movements.

6. Personal Development and Self-Improvement: Pursuits such as personal growth, productivity, motivation, goal-setting, and success strategies.

7. Travel and Adventure: Exploring new destinations, unique experiences, adventure sports, and discovering different cultures.

8. Food and Culinary Experiences: Unique and diverse cuisines, cooking techniques, food trends, and culinary exploration.

9. Financial Education and Investment: Building wealth, financial literacy, investment strategies, and personal finance management.

10. Science and Space Exploration: Discoveries, breakthroughs, space missions, and scientific exploration.

Remember that individual interests may vary, and what captures the attention of one person may not resonate with another. It's essential to consider your target audience and their specific interests when tailoring content or products.

Why Should I Invest in Night Cafe Images Right Now?

There are several compelling reasons to consider buying Night Cafe images right now. Firstly, these images offer a captivating and unique visual aesthetic that can add depth and beauty to a wide range of creative projects. Whether you're designing book covers, creating artwork, or developing merchandise, Night Cafe images can bring an element of intrigue and inspiration. Secondly, the versatility of Night Cafe images allows for countless applications across various mediums and industries, including graphic design, home decor, fashion, and more. Their timeless appeal and artistic quality make them suitable for both contemporary and classic designs. Additionally, investing in

Night Cafe images provides an opportunity to tap into a growing demand for visually striking and engaging content in the digital age. As visual media becomes increasingly prevalent, having access to high-quality, captivating images can help your projects stand out and resonate with your audience. Lastly, by purchasing Night Cafe images, you support the talented artists behind these creations, enabling them to continue producing remarkable visual works that inspire and captivate.

To get started with Night Cafe images, realize that there is no "right" way to start. Just let your interest and your personal enthusiasm carry you forward. You can't go wrong. All roads lead to marketing.

That's it for now — this will give you a bit of work to do in your morning meeting, for sure. There's a lot to work with and a lot to get familiar with, particularly the niche-marketing and creation of the ideal image and caption for each item you try to sell.

How To Sell Stuff

I Have Cups Like Some People Have Mice!

Introducing our E.J. Gold Art Mugs, where creativity meets functionality! Elevate your coffee or tea drinking experience with these stunning mugs that showcase the beauty of art. Here's why our E.J. Gold Art Mugs on Zazzle are a must-have:

1. Artistic Masterpieces: Each mug is adorned with carefully curated artwork by E.J. Gold, a renowned artist with a captivating vision. From mesmerizing landscapes to captivating abstract designs, our collection offers a diverse range of E.J. Gold's artistic styles that will delight and inspire. Start your day with a dose of E.J. Gold's artistic beauty in your hands.

2. Express Your Personal Style: Our E.J. Gold Art Mugs are not just ordinary drink ware; they are an extension of your unique personality and style. Whether you prefer bold and vibrant colors or elegant and minimalist designs, we have an E.J. Gold mug that reflects your individuality. Sip your favorite beverage in a mug that speaks to your aesthetic taste.

3. High-Quality Craftsmanship: We take pride in delivering mugs of exceptional quality. Each E.J. Gold mug is meticulously crafted using durable materials, ensuring long-lasting use and resistance to everyday wear and tear. With their sturdy build and comfortable grip, our mugs are designed to be your trusty companions for countless sips of enjoyment.

4. Perfect for Gifting: Looking for a thoughtful and unique gift? Look no further than our E.J. Gold Art Mugs. Whether it's for birthdays, anniversaries, or any special occasion, these mugs make a memorable and personal present for art enthusiasts and coffee lovers alike. Show your loved ones that you appreciate their individuality with a gift that celebrates E.J. Gold's passion for art.

5. Functional Art: Not only do our E.J. Gold mugs showcase breathtaking artwork, but they are also highly functional. With their spacious capacity and comfortable handles, they are perfect for enjoying your morning coffee, indulging in a soothing cup of tea, or savoring a delicious hot chocolate. Experience the harmony of art and functionality in every sip.

Experience the magic of art with our E.J. Gold Art Mugs. Whether you're adding them to your collection, expressing your style, or gifting them to someone special, these mugs are a celebration of E.J. Gold's creativity and taste. Choose your favorite design and start your day with E.J. Gold's art in your hands.

Fourth-Way Buttons!

Hey, guess what? I'm selling these super cool buttons with the "4th Way" slogan! You won't believe why people would want to buy them. Check it out:

It's all about expressing who you are. These buttons let people show off their support for the "4th Way" philosophy. It's like wearing your beliefs on your sleeve (or, well, on your shirt)!

Imagine this: you're wearing one of these buttons, and someone notices. Boom! Instant conversation starter. You'll get people curious, asking questions, and maybe even finding common ground. It's a fantastic way to connect with like-minded folks.

It's not just about looking cool — it's about feeling like you belong. When you wear these buttons, you're signaling that you're part of a community, a movement. It's a way to find your tribe and be among friends who share similar values.

You know what's awesome? By rocking one of these buttons, you're showing support and advocating for the "4th Way" ideology. It's a way to make a statement. You might even inspire others to explore this philosophy and join the cause!

And let's not forget the fashion factor. These buttons aren't just meaningful; they're also trendy accessories. The design is top-notch, with catchy colors and an overall stylish look. Who wouldn't want to add that extra flair to their outfit?

So, that's why these "4th Way" buttons are a must-have. They're not just buttons — they're a way to express yourself, connect with others, and make a statement in style. Isn't that awesome?

Acrylic Cutouts

Introducing stunning acrylic cutout sculptures, crafted from my original designs! These one-of-a-kind art pieces are a must-have for art enthusiasts and collectors alike. Here's why you'll love them:

1. Unique Design: Each sculpture is meticulously crafted from my original designs, making them truly unique and unlike anything you'll find elsewhere. They showcase my artistic vision and attention to detail, ensuring you own a truly special piece of art.

2. Captivating Visual Impact: The use of acrylic material adds a captivating element to these sculptures. The interplay of light and transparency creates an enchanting visual experience, transforming any space into a gallery-like showcase.

3. Versatile Decor: Whether it's for your home, office, or as a gift, these sculptures add a touch of elegance and sophistication to any setting. They effortlessly blend with various interior styles, making them a versatile choice for any decor theme.

4. Conversation Starters: These sculptures serve as conversation starters, drawing the attention and admiration of art enthusiasts. Showcase your unique taste and spark intriguing discussions with visitors, colleagues, or friends who appreciate exceptional artistry.

5. Premium Quality: Made with high-quality acrylic material, these sculptures are built to last. The durable and resilient nature of acrylic ensures your investment remains stunning and intact, bringing years of artistic joy.

Don't miss the opportunity to own these remarkable acrylic cutout sculptures. Experience the beauty of original designs and elevate your space with a touch of artistic brilliance. Start your art collection today!

Unleash Your Bardo Memory!

Introducing "Godd Games," where vintage meets cutting-edge technology for an unforgettable gaming experience! Prepare to embark on a journey like no other, where nostalgia blends seamlessly with modern advancements. Here's why you'll be captivated by these unique PC games:

1. Retro-Inspired, Technologically Advanced: "Godd Games" beautifully combines the charm of early video games with state-of-the-art technology. Immerse yourself in pixelated landscapes and classic game play mechanics, all enhanced by the power of modern graphics and performance. It's a nostalgic adventure brought to life like never before!

2. Unleash Bardo Memory: Get ready to explore the realms beyond with "Godd Games." The architecture, colors, and fog effects are carefully designed to trigger Bardo Memory—an awakening and awareness that connects you to the afterlife. Experience a captivating journey that goes beyond traditional gaming, opening your mind to new dimensions of thought and reflection.

3. Engaging Game play: These games are not just visually stunning; they offer immersive and engaging game play that will keep you hooked for hours. Discover intricate puzzles, challenging quests, and unique storytelling that will captivate your senses and leave you craving for more. It's an adventure that will transport you to a world both familiar and extraordinary.

4. Retro Comfort: While "Godd Games" embrace the retro aesthetic, they also prioritize your modern comfort. Experience seamless controls, customizable settings, and a user-friendly interface that ensures an enjoyable gaming experience. Dive into the nostalgic world without sacrificing convenience or ease of play.

5. Collectible Masterpieces: These games aren't just entertainment; they're collectible masterpieces. Each title is thoughtfully crafted with attention to detail, making them coveted items for gaming enthusiasts and collectors. Build your personal "Godd Games" collection and be part of a community that appreciates the artistry and craftsmanship behind these timeless creations.

Immerse yourself in the fusion of vintage nostalgia and cutting-edge technology. Unleash Bardo Memory, solve captivating puzzles, and experience gaming like never before. Discover the allure of "Godd Games" and let your journey begin!

Remember to adapt and customize the sales pitch to align with your specific audience and promotional channels. Best of luck with your campaign, and may your "Godd Games" find their way into the hearts of gamers everywhere!

Dragon 3D is Here!

Introducing Dragon 3D, the ultimate fusion of challenge, retro charm, and cutting-edge technology! Get ready for an unforgettable gaming experience that sets itself apart from the rest. Here's why Dragon 3D will leave you breathless:

1. A Retro Challenge Reborn: Dragon 3D takes inspiration from classic games like Dragon Killer, delivering a nostalgic experience that will transport you back to the golden age of gaming. Brace yourself for intense battles, cunning enemies, and epic quests that will test your skills to the limit. It's a thrilling homage to the past, revitalized for the present.

2. Unleash the Power of Cutting-Edge Technology: What sets Dragon 3D apart is its foundation on the most highly developed game engine in the world. Witness the seamless integration of stunning visuals, realistic physics, and immersive soundscapes that breathe life into the game's vibrant world. It's the perfect blend of retro aesthetics and advanced technology, delivering an unparalleled gaming experience.

3. Master the Art of Strategy: Dragon 3D isn't just about reflexes; it's a game that rewards tactical thinking and careful planning. Uncover hidden secrets, forge alliances, and make critical decisions that will shape your journey. Prepare to dive deep into an intricate world filled with intriguing characters, captivating lore, and morally challenging dilemmas. The fate of the realm lies in your hands.

4. Endless Adventure, Infinite Possibilities: Immerse yourself in Dragon 3D's vast open world, where every corner holds new discoveries and untold treasures. Engage in exhilarating combat, harness powerful magic, and embark on quests that will push your limits. Whether you choose the path of a valiant hero or a cunning rogue, the adventure awaits, with endless possibilities for exploration and growth.

5. Embrace the Call of the Dragon: With Dragon 3D, you're not just playing a game — you're embracing a mythical legacy. Experience the awe-inspiring presence of majestic dragons, forge unbreakable bonds with them, and wield their powers as you face epic showdowns. Unleash your inner dragon slayer and leave a mark on the annals of gaming history.

Gear up for an unforgettable quest in Dragon 3D, where retro challenge meets the pinnacle of technological innovation. Are you ready to embark on a journey that will test your mettle and ignite your gaming passion? The dragons await your call!

The thing is, you can make and sell things, too! Get on it and get with it! So here's a bonus setup for you to help you create a business cycle for yourself:

Selling Your Nightcafe Images on Zazzle and Etsy

Introduction: Welcome, everyone! Today, we'll be discussing an exciting topic for artists and photographers: selling your Nightcafe images online. With the rise of e-commerce platforms, such as Zazzle and Etsy, you have incredible opportunities to showcase your work to a global audience and turn your passion into a profitable venture. In this lecture, we'll explore the benefits and features of Zazzle and Etsy, and learn how you can effectively leverage these platforms to sell your Nightcafe images.

I.   Zazzle — Unleashing Your Creativity:

A. Zazzle Overview: Zazzle is an online marketplace that allows artists, designers, and photographers to create and sell their unique products. It offers a vast range of customizable items, including clothing, home decor, accessories, and more.

B. Getting Started:

1. Set up an Account: Visit the Zazzle website and create an account to get started.

2. Design Your Nightcafe Collection: Use Zazzle's design tools to create captivating products featuring your Nightcafe images.

3. Product Selection: Choose the items you want to sell, such as prints, posters, mugs, or even smartphone cases.

C. Customization and Personalization:

1. Customizable Templates: Zazzle provides templates for each product, allowing you to add your Nightcafe images and personalize them with text, colors, and additional graphics.
2. Product Previews: Ensure your designs look great by using the preview feature to see how they will appear on different products.

D. Promoting Your Products:

1. Zazzle Storefront: Create a customized storefront to showcase your Nightcafe collection and make it easy for customers to browse and purchase your products.
2. Social Media and Marketing: Leverage social media platforms and other marketing strategies to drive traffic to your Zazzle store and increase sales.

Etsy — Building an Artistic Brand:
A. Etsy Overview: Etsy is a popular online marketplace focused on handmade and vintage items, making it an ideal platform for artists and photographers to sell their Nightcafe images.

B. Setting Up Your Shop:

1. Account Creation: Sign up for an Etsy seller account and choose a memorable shop name.
2. Shop Policies: Establish clear shop policies regarding shipping, returns, and customer service.

C. Listing Your Nightcafe Images:

1. High-Quality Images: Capture professional-quality photographs of your Nightcafe artwork to make a lasting impression on potential buyers.
2. Compelling Descriptions: Write detailed, engaging descriptions that highlight the story behind each piece and evoke emotions.

D. Storefront Customization:

1. Shop Banner and Logo: Design an attractive banner and logo that reflects the essence of your Nightcafe collection.
2. Sections and Categories: Organize your shop into relevant sections and categories to help customers navigate your listings more efficiently.

E. Building Your Brand:

1. Consistency: Maintain a consistent style and theme across your listings and shop to develop a recognizable brand.
2. Customer Interaction: Provide excellent customer service and promptly respond to inquiries and feedback.

Conclusion: Selling your Nightcafe images online can be a fulfilling and profitable endeavor. By utilizing platforms like Zazzle and Etsy, you can reach a vast audience, showcase your unique artwork, and build a brand around your Nightcafe collection. Remember to explore the customization options, effectively market your products, and provide exceptional customer service. Good luck on your journey as you turn your passion into a thriving business!

Death & Dying for Beginners

The ultimate apres-vie videogame, is now available as a download.

Death & Dying for Beginners:

Discover the profound journey of life's final chapter at our transformative workshop on 'Death & Dying For Beginners'. Here's a template for you to use to create your own sense of excitement about the upcoming workshops!

Join us for a thought-provoking exploration into the universal aspects of mortality, offering valuable insights and empowering perspectives on this often misunderstood topic. This workshop aims to foster a greater understanding of death and dying, allowing participants to approach these profound experiences with compassion, knowledge, and emotional resilience.

Through engaging discussions, expert-led sessions, and interactive activities, you'll gain a fresh perspective on mortality, end-of-life planning, and the potential for personal growth amidst life's impermanence. Our experienced facilitators will guide you through a range of topics, including:

1. Navigating grief and loss: Emotionally healthy approaches to processing and honoring the loss of loved ones.
2. Advance care planning: Practical tools and resources to ensure your end-of-life wishes are known and respected.
3. Cultivating resilience: Building emotional strength and finding meaning in the face of mortality.
4. Cultural perspectives on death: Exploring diverse traditions and rituals surrounding death and dying.

Whether you're a healthcare professional, caregiver, or simply seeking personal growth, this workshop provides a safe and supportive space to engage in meaningful conversations and expand your understanding of this inevitable part of life.

Join us on [Date] at [Location] to embark on a transformative journey towards embracing the beauty and complexities of mortality. Limited spots are available, so secure your place today and embark on a path towards compassionate awareness.

[Registration details/contact information]

Embrace the wisdom of mortality. Begin your journey today.

I hope you put that to good use. I did. If you don't, who will?

Most Popular Calendars

Most Popular Calendars:

1. Wildlife and Nature Calendars: These calendars feature stunning illustrations and photographs of various animals, birds, landscapes, and natural wonders. I'm currently working on an alien wildlife calendar.

2. Art and Artists Calendars: These calendars showcase famous artworks or highlight the works of renowned artists, featuring a different masterpiece each month.

3. Travel and Adventure Calendars: These calendars take you on a visual journey to different destinations, featuring breathtaking landscapes, iconic landmarks, and cultural experiences.

4. Sports Calendars: Sports-themed calendars cater to fans of various sports, featuring action shots, athletes, and important events in the sports world.

5. Food and Drink Calendars: These calendars celebrate culinary delights, showcasing appetizing dishes, recipes, and food-related themes.

6. Pop Culture and Entertainment Calendars: These calendars feature illustrations and photographs of celebrities, movie posters, TV shows, or popular cultural references.

7. Inspirational and Motivational Calendars: These calendars focus on inspiring quotes, positive affirmations, and uplifting illustrations to keep you motivated throughout the year.

8. Music Calendars: Music-themed calendars often highlight musicians, bands, album covers, or music genres, offering a visual tribute to the world of music.

9. History and Heritage Calendars: These calendars showcase historical events, iconic figures, or heritage sites, offering glimpses into the past and cultural significance.

10. Science and Space Calendars: For science enthusiasts, these calendars feature illustrations of scientific discoveries, space exploration, astronomy, and cosmic wonders.

Wildlife & Nature Calendars:

Wildlife and Nature Calendars are incredibly popular and widely loved for their stunning illustrations and photographs of the natural world. Here are some subcategories within this subject matter:

1.1. Animals of the World: These calendars feature a diverse range of animals from different continents and ecosystems. You can expect to see captivating illustrations or high-quality photographs of mammals, birds, reptiles, amphibians, and marine life.

1.2. Birds and Birdwatching: Bird lovers enjoy calendars that focus specifically on birds, showcasing different species, their habitats, and behaviors. These calendars often include detailed illustrations or photographs capturing the beauty of these feathered creatures.

1.3. Wildlife Conservation: Some calendars within this category aim to raise awareness about wildlife conservation efforts. They may highlight endangered species, conservation projects, or showcase the work of wildlife photographers who capture unique moments in the animal kingdom.

1.4. National Parks and Landscapes: Calendars featuring national parks and landscapes are popular among nature enthusiasts and travelers. They showcase breathtaking vistas, scenic landscapes, and iconic natural wonders found within specific regions or countries.

1.5. Seasons and Botanical Illustrations: These calendars often celebrate the changing seasons and the beauty of flora and fauna. You can expect to find intricate illustrations or photographs showcasing flowers, plants, trees, and the vibrant colors associated with each season.

1.6. Underwater World: For those fascinated by marine life and the wonders beneath the sea, underwater-themed calendars offer mesmerizing illustrations or photographs of coral reefs, colorful fish, exotic creatures, and underwater ecosystems.

These are just a few examples of the diverse range of wildlife and nature calendars available. Each calendar typically features a different illustration or photograph for each month, allowing you to enjoy the beauty of the natural world throughout the year.

Art & Artists Calendars:

Art and Artists Calendars are highly popular among art enthusiasts and those who appreciate the beauty and creativity of visual arts. These calendars often feature a different artwork or artist each month, allowing you to immerse yourself in the world of art throughout the year. Here are some subcategories within this subject matter:

2.1. Famous Artists: Calendars in this category showcase the works of renowned artists from various periods and art movements. Each month might feature a masterpiece from artists like Leonardo da Vinci, Vincent van Gogh, Pablo Picasso, Claude Monet, Salvador Dalí, or Frida Kahlo, to name just a few.

2.2. Art Movements and Styles: These calendars focus on specific art movements or styles, offering a visual journey through art history. You might find calendars dedicated to Impressionism, Cubism, Surrealism, Abstract Expressionism, Renaissance, or Pop Art, among others.

2.3. Modern and Contemporary Art: For those interested in the latest trends and contemporary artists, calendars featuring modern and contemporary art are popular. They might include works from emerging artists or highlight influential figures in the current art scene.

2.4. Museum Collections: Some calendars feature artworks from specific museums or art collections. These calendars can provide a glimpse into the vast range of artworks housed in renowned institutions like the Louvre, Metropolitan Museum of Art, Tate Modern, or the Guggenheim Museum.

2.5. Artistic Themes: Calendars focusing on specific artistic themes are also available. These may include calendars dedicated to landscapes, still life, portraiture, abstract art, or genre-specific themes like nautical art, floral art, or cityscapes.

2.6. Art Techniques: Some calendars explore various art techniques or mediums, providing insights into different artistic processes. For example, you might find calendars showcasing watercolor paintings, oil paintings, pastel drawings, or mixed media artworks.

Art and Artists Calendars are not only visually appealing but also provide an opportunity to learn about different artists, their styles, and the significance of their works. They are a perfect choice for art lovers or anyone looking to add a touch of creativity to their living or working space.

Travel & Adventure Calendars:

Travel and Adventure Calendars. These calendars take you on a visual journey to different destinations, offering glimpses of breathtaking landscapes, iconic landmarks, and cultural experiences. Here are some subcategories within this subject matter:

3.1. Countries and Regions: Calendars dedicated to specific countries or regions showcase the beauty and diversity of their landscapes, architecture, and cultural heritage. Whether it's calendars focusing on Italy, France, Japan, or Africa, you can expect stunning photographs or illustrations highlighting the unique aspects of each place.

3.2. Cityscapes: City-themed calendars capture the essence of famous cities around the world. They showcase iconic landmarks, skylines, and architectural marvels, allowing you to explore urban environments and experience the atmosphere of cities like New York, Paris, London, Tokyo, or Dubai.

3.3. Natural Wonders: Calendars in this category feature awe-inspiring natural landscapes and wonders. From majestic mountains and cascading waterfalls to serene beaches and lush forests, these calendars transport you to some of the most beautiful natural locations on the planet, such as the Grand Canyon, the Amazon Rainforest, the Great Barrier Reef, or the Northern Lights.

3.4. Adventure and Outdoor Pursuits: These calendars celebrate the spirit of adventure and outdoor activities. They often feature thrilling sports like rock climbing, hiking, kayaking, skiing, or surfing, showcasing adrenaline-pumping moments in stunning natural settings.

3.5. UNESCO World Heritage Sites: Calendars dedicated to UNESCO World Heritage Sites highlight the cultural and historical significance of these protected locations. They offer glimpses into ancient ruins, archaeological sites, and architectural masterpieces that have earned recognition and preservation by UNESCO.

3.6. Travel Photography: Some calendars feature captivating travel photographs taken by talented photographers. These calendars offer a collection of stunning images from around the world, capturing the beauty of landscapes, people, and cultures across different continents.

Travel and Adventure Calendars are a great way to visually explore the world and inspire wanderlust. They make fantastic gifts for travel enthusiasts or serve as a reminder to plan your next adventure.

Sports Calendars:

Sports Calendars. These calendars are highly popular among sports enthusiasts and fans who enjoy following their favorite sports, athletes, and teams. They offer a visual celebration of the world of sports and often feature dynamic action shots, iconic moments, and important events. Here are some subcategories within this subject matter:

4.1. Major Sports: Calendars dedicated to major sports like football (soccer), basketball, baseball, American football, tennis, or rugby are widely available. They showcase key moments from popular leagues, tournaments, or championships, featuring star players and memorable plays.

4.2. Individual Sports: Some calendars focus on individual sports such as golf, tennis, athletics, swimming, or boxing. These calendars may feature exceptional athletes, record-breaking achievements, or iconic moments specific to each sport.

4.3. Team Sports: Calendars dedicated to team sports like basketball, football, ice hockey, or cricket highlight the camaraderie, teamwork, and competitive spirit of these sports. They often feature team photographs, action shots, and notable events from the season.

4.4. Olympic Sports: With the Olympic Games being a global celebration of sports, calendars dedicated to Olympic sports are quite popular. These calendars showcase a wide range of sports, from swimming and gymnastics to track and field, providing a comprehensive visual overview of the Olympic movement.

4.5. Legends and Hall of Famers: Some calendars pay tribute to legendary athletes and Hall of Famers who have made a significant impact on their respective sports. They feature iconic photographs and memorable moments from the careers of sports legends, honoring their contributions to the sporting world.

4.6. Sports Illustrated Moments: Calendars inspired by publications like Sports Illustrated capture some of the most iconic moments in sports history. They feature famous photographs that have graced the pages of sports magazines, highlighting moments of triumph, emotion, and athleticism.

These sports calendars are a great way to stay connected with your favorite sports and athletes throughout the year. They make fantastic gifts for sports fans or serve as a source of inspiration and motivation for those involved in sports themselves.

Food & Drink Calendars:

Food and Drink Calendars. These calendars celebrate the culinary world, showcasing appetizing dishes, recipes, and food-related themes. They are popular among food enthusiasts, home cooks, and anyone with an appreciation for gastronomy. Here are some subcategories within this subject matter:

5.1. Food Photography: Calendars featuring food photography are visually appealing and showcase beautifully styled dishes. Each month may highlight a mouthwatering recipe or focus on a particular cuisine, using vibrant colors and artistic compositions to capture the essence of the food.

5.2. Recipe Calendars: These calendars feature a different recipe each month, providing inspiration for home cooking. They often include step-by-step instructions, ingredient lists, and tantalizing images of the finished dish, encouraging you to try new recipes and expand your culinary skills.

5.3. Cuisine-Specific Calendars: Calendars dedicated to specific cuisines are popular among those who have a particular affinity for a certain style of cooking. Whether it's Italian, Asian, Mexican, Mediterranean, or any other cuisine, these calendars highlight the flavors, ingredients, and culinary traditions associated with each cuisine.

5.4. Desserts and Baking: For those with a sweet tooth, dessert-themed calendars are a delight. They showcase delectable desserts, pastries, and baked goods, providing inspiration for indulgent treats throughout the year. These calendars may also include baking tips, seasonal dessert ideas, or profiles of renowned pastry chefs.

5.5. Wine and Spirits: Calendars focusing on wine and spirits are popular among wine enthusiasts and connoisseurs. They feature vineyards, wine regions, tasting notes, and recommendations for pairing food with different wines. Some calendars may also highlight the world of craft cocktails and mixology.

5.6. Food and Travel: These calendars combine the love of food and travel, showcasing culinary experiences from around the world. They may feature iconic street foods, famous restaurants, food markets, or traditional dishes associated with different countries and cultures.

Food and Drink Calendars not only serve as decorative pieces but also offer inspiration, new recipes, and a visual feast for the senses. They make great gifts for food lovers or serve as a reminder to explore the diverse and delicious world of cuisine throughout the year.

Pop Culture & Entertainment:

Pop Culture and Entertainment Calendars. These calendars cater to fans of popular culture and offer a visual tribute to various forms of entertainment. They often feature illustrations, photographs, or artwork related to celebrities, movies, TV shows, or other cultural references. Here are some subcategories within this subject matter:

6.1. Celebrity Calendars: These calendars focus on renowned celebrities from the world of entertainment, including actors, actresses, musicians, and public figures. Each month may feature a different celebrity, showcasing their portraits, iconic looks, or memorable moments from their careers.

6.2. Movie Calendars: Movie-themed calendars celebrate the world of cinema, featuring posters, stills, or artwork from popular films. They may highlight a specific movie genre, franchise, or pay tribute to classic movies and iconic characters.

6.3. TV Show Calendars: TV show-themed calendars cater to fans of beloved television series. They often feature images or illustrations of the show's characters, memorable scenes, or references to iconic episodes, providing a nostalgic or current connection to the world of television.

6.4. Music Calendars: These calendars celebrate the world of music, showcasing musicians, bands, or music genres. They may feature photographs, album covers, or illustrations of artists and highlight significant events in the music industry.

6.5. Comic and Animation Calendars: Calendars dedicated to comic books, graphic novels, or animated series feature illustrations, artwork, or scenes from popular franchises. They cater to fans of superheroes, manga, anime, or other forms of illustrated storytelling.

6.6. Gaming Calendars: Gaming-themed calendars cater to video game enthusiasts, featuring artwork, characters, or scenes from popular games. They may showcase upcoming game releases, notable anniversaries, or iconic moments in gaming history.

Pop Culture and Entertainment Calendars allow fans to display their passion for their favorite celebrities, movies, TV shows, music, or gaming. They make great gifts for fans or serve as a visual reminder of the entertainment world's impact and influence throughout the year.

Inspirational & Motivational:

Inspirational and Motivational Calendars. These calendars are designed to inspire, uplift, and provide daily doses of positivity and motivation. They often feature quotes, affirmations, and beautiful illustrations or photographs that encourage personal growth and well-being. Here are some subcategories within this subject matter:

7.1. Quotes and Affirmations: Calendars in this category feature inspirational quotes, affirmations, or mantras that aim to uplift and motivate. Each month may present a different quote or affirmation, accompanied by complementary artwork or imagery.

7.2. Mindfulness and Self-Care: These calendars emphasize the importance of self-care and mindfulness. They may include reminders to practice gratitude, meditation, or other self-care techniques. The calendars may also offer tips for achieving balance and well-being in daily life.

7.3. Goal Setting and Productivity: Calendars focused on goal setting and productivity encourage users to set and achieve their personal or professional goals. They may include prompts, action steps, or motivational messages that support progress and growth throughout the year.

7.4. Personal Development and Success: These calendars aim to inspire personal development and success. They may feature quotes from influential figures in various fields, stories of triumph, or strategies for overcoming challenges and achieving goals.

7.5. Inspirational Stories and Role Models: Calendars in this category share inspiring stories of resilience, triumph, and notable figures who have made a positive impact. Each month may highlight a different individual or group, celebrating their achievements and contributions.

7.6. Nature and Wellness: Calendars in this subcategory combine inspiration with nature and wellness themes. They may feature calming landscapes, serene natural settings, or reminders to connect with the outdoors and prioritize well-being.

Inspirational and Motivational Calendars serve as a daily reminder to stay positive, focused, and motivated. They can be an excellent addition to personal spaces, offices, or as thoughtful gifts for individuals seeking encouragement and inspiration in their daily lives.

Music Calendars:

Music Calendars: These calendars are dedicated to the world of music, showcasing musicians, bands, instruments, and musical themes. They cater to music lovers and fans of various genres. Here are some subcategories within this subject matter:

8.1. Band and Artist Calendars: These calendars focus on specific bands or artists, featuring photographs, artwork, or illustrations of the musicians. Each month may highlight a different band member or present iconic images associated with the artist's career.

8.2. Genre-specific Calendars: Calendars dedicated to specific music genres celebrate the unique sounds and styles associated with each genre. They may focus on genres like rock, jazz, hip-hop, classical, country, electronic, or pop, featuring relevant imagery and symbols associated with the genre.

8.3. Music Festivals and Concerts: Calendars in this category highlight music festivals, concerts, or live performances. They may feature photographs or illustrations of famous music festivals, stages, or memorable moments from concerts, offering a visual journey through the vibrant world of live music.

8.4. Instruments and Musicians: These calendars celebrate the beauty and craftsmanship of musical instruments. They may feature close-up photographs or artistic illustrations of instruments like guitars, pianos, drums, violins, or brass instruments, paying tribute to the artistry of musicians.

8.5. Album Covers and Artwork: Calendars featuring album covers and artwork showcase iconic designs and imagery associated with music albums. They may highlight influential albums or present a collection of memorable album covers, serving as a visual homage to music history.

8.6. Music Quotes and Lyrics: Some music calendars feature inspiring quotes or memorable song lyrics from renowned musicians. They provide daily doses of musical inspiration and serve as a reminder of the power of music to uplift and connect people.

Music Calendars celebrate the universal language of music and allow fans to connect with their favorite artists, genres, or musical experiences throughout the year. They make great gifts for music enthusiasts, musicians, or anyone who appreciates the transformative power of music.

History & Heritage Calendars:

History and Heritage Calendars: These calendars delve into the rich tapestry of history, culture, and heritage, offering glimpses into significant events, historical figures, and iconic landmarks. They provide an opportunity to explore and appreciate the diverse narratives and legacies of various civilizations. Here are some subcategories within this subject matter:

9.1. Historical Events: Calendars focused on historical events highlight key moments in history, such as important battles, revolutions, discoveries, or significant milestones. Each month may feature a different event, accompanied by relevant images, dates, and brief descriptions.

9.2. Historical Figures: These calendars pay tribute to influential historical figures who have made a lasting impact on society. They may feature portraits, photographs, or illustrations of notable individuals from various fields, including politics, art, science, literature, and more.

9.3. Cultural Celebrations: Calendars celebrating cultural heritage showcase important festivals, traditions, or celebrations from around the world. They provide insights into diverse cultures and may feature colorful photographs, illustrations, or artwork associated with these cultural events.

9.4. Heritage Sites and Landmarks: Calendars dedicated to heritage sites and landmarks highlight iconic places with historical or cultural significance. They may feature photographs or artistic renderings of UNESCO World Heritage Sites, ancient monuments, architectural marvels, or places of cultural importance.

9.5. Historical Art and Artifacts: These calendars showcase historical art, artifacts, and antiquities. They may feature images or illustrations of famous paintings, sculptures, historical documents, or ancient artifacts, providing a visual exploration of artistic and historical treasures.

9.6. Time Periods and Eras: Calendars that focus on specific time periods or eras provide a comprehensive overview of the historical context, developments, and cultural shifts during those times. They may feature images, artwork, or illustrations that represent the spirit and essence of the respective era.

History and Heritage Calendars offer a fascinating journey through time and serve as a reminder of the significance of our collective history and cultural heritage. They are ideal for history enthusiasts, travelers, or anyone interested in exploring the stories and legacies of civilizations from around the world.

Science & Space Calendars:

Science and Space Calendars: These calendars delve into the wonders of scientific discoveries, space exploration, and the mysteries of the universe. They cater to science enthusiasts, astronomy lovers, and those with a curiosity for the natural world. Here are some subcategories within this subject matter:

10.1. Astronomy and Space Exploration: Calendars dedicated to astronomy and space exploration showcase captivating photographs, illustrations, or artwork of celestial objects, such as stars, galaxies, planets, and nebulae. They may feature images captured by telescopes or spacecraft, highlighting cosmic wonders.

10.2. Scientific Concepts and Phenomena: These calendars explore scientific concepts, theories, and phenomena, making complex subjects more accessible and engaging. They may feature visual representations, diagrams, or illustrations that explain topics such as physics, biology, chemistry, or environmental science.

10.3. Scientific Achievements and Discoveries: Calendars in this category celebrate notable scientific achievements and discoveries throughout history. They may feature profiles of influential scientists, descriptions of groundbreaking experiments, or illustrations representing significant scientific breakthroughs.

10.4. Natural Sciences and Earth Sciences: These calendars focus on the natural world and Earth sciences. They may feature images or illustrations showcasing geological formations, ecosystems, weather patterns, or the diversity of flora and fauna on our planet.

10.5. Space Missions and Astronauts: Calendars dedicated to space missions and astronauts highlight notable missions, spacecraft, or astronauts who have ventured into space. They may feature photographs, artwork, or illustrations capturing the excitement and challenges of space exploration.

10.6. Scientific Events and Anniversaries: Some calendars highlight significant scientific events, conferences, or anniversaries throughout the year. They provide information on important dates in scientific history, honoring scientific milestones and breakthroughs.

Science and Space Calendars offer a fascinating glimpse into the mysteries of the universe, scientific progress, and the wonders of our planet. They inspire curiosity, awe, and a deeper understanding of the natural world and our place within it. These calendars are ideal for science enthusiasts, students, educators, and anyone with a passion for exploration and discovery.

Yes, I know it's overly long, but I wanted to get all the information together on one page, in one single easily scanned list, and that's why I done what I done.

I hope this serves you well in your quest for better calendars! We'll tackle other applications of your generative art in later blogs.

Just one more item, something I just came up with on my own, which means "tapping into the cosmic constant":

Introducing the innovative Calendar Coloring Book — a perfect blend of functionality and creativity! This unique calendar offers an exciting and interactive experience that will delight both children and adults alike. Here's our sales pitch for this captivating product:

"Unleash your creativity and stay organized with our Calendar Coloring Book! It's not just an ordinary calendar; it's a coloring adventure that combines practicality with artistic expression. Imagine a calendar that not only helps you keep track of important dates but also serves as a delightful coloring book, allowing you to create a personalized masterpiece every month.

With our Calendar Coloring Book, each month presents a beautifully illustrated design waiting to be brought to life with vibrant colors. Whether you prefer intricate patterns, whimsical illustrations, or captivating landscapes, our calendar offers a variety of themes to suit your artistic taste.

Children will love the joy of coloring and exploring their imagination as they mark special occasions on the calendar. It's a wonderful way to engage their creativity while teaching them the importance of time management and organization. Parents and teachers will appreciate the opportunity to combine fun and learning in one convenient package.

For adults, our Calendar Coloring Book provides a therapeutic and relaxing experience. Coloring has been proven to reduce stress and promote mindfulness. Take a break from the busy world, grab your favorite coloring tools, and immerse yourself in the calming artistry of each month's design. Plus, it's a fantastic way to add a personal touch to your living or working space.

But that's not all! Our Calendar Coloring Book is made with high-quality paper, ensuring that your colors glide smoothly and that your artistic creations will stand the test of time. Each page is conveniently perforated, making it easy to tear out and display your finished artwork proudly.

Whether you're looking for a thoughtful gift for a loved one or a delightful treat for yourself, our Calendar Coloring Book is the perfect choice. It combines practicality, creativity, and a touch of whimsy, making every day a chance to unleash your inner artist.

Don't miss out on this extraordinary calendar that offers so much more than just dates. Embrace the joy of coloring, stay organized, and make every month an artistic adventure with our Calendar Coloring Book. Order yours today and let your creativity soar!"

With this sales pitch, you can effectively highlight the unique features and benefits of the Calendar Coloring Book, emphasizing its ability to bring joy, creativity, and organization together in a single product.

Brushstrokes of Brilliance

You can paint this baby bodysuit!

Unleash Your Inner Artist: Transform Any Item into a Personalized Coloring Book! Are you ready to embark on a creative adventure unlike any other? Introducing our innovative Coloring Book Creator Kit, where you have the power to turn any item into a canvas for your imagination!

With our kit, the possibilities are endless. Here's why you'll love becoming a coloring book creator:

1. Endless creativity: Set your imagination free and breathe new life into everyday items. Whether it's a plain t-shirt, a simple tote bag, or even a blank notebook, you can transform them into personalized coloring books, adding vibrancy and character to your world.

2. Customized masterpieces: Express your unique style by designing intricate line art patterns that reflect your personality. Create themed coloring books for different occasions, personalized gifts for loved ones, or simply indulge in the joy of designing one-of-a-kind art pieces. It's an opportunity to unleash your creativity in ways you never thought possible.

3. Relaxation and mindfulness: Coloring has long been hailed as a therapeutic and calming activity. By transforming items into coloring books, you can enjoy moments of tranquility and mindfulness as you fill each page with beautiful colors. It's a meditative experience that brings joy, peace, and a sense of accomplishment.

4. Family fun and bonding: Gather your loved ones for hours of creative enjoyment. From children to grandparents, everyone can join in the coloring book craze. It's a wonderful opportunity to connect, share stories, and create lasting memories together.

5. Unique entrepreneurial ventures: Are you an aspiring artist or entrepreneur? Our Coloring Book Creator Kit opens up a world of business opportunities. Design and sell customized coloring books, offer workshops, or create a brand around your artistic creations. It's a chance to turn your passion into a thriving venture.

The Coloring Book Creator Kit: Ignite your imagination and unlock a world of creativity! Start transforming everyday items into personalized coloring books today. Embrace the joy of self-expression, relaxation, and endless artistic possibilities. Unleash your inner artist and let your colors soar!

Get your Coloring Book Creator Kit now and embark on a colorful journey like never before!

But wait! There's more!

Unleashing Your Inner Painter!

Did you know? We have an exciting new workshop that will unleash your inner artist and teach you how to create stunning painted articles!

Discover the magic of painting adorable baby bodysuits, adding a personalized touch to each little masterpiece. From cute animals to playful patterns, you'll learn techniques to bring vibrant colors to life on these tiny canvases. It's a creative journey that combines joy and style!

And that's not all! Join our workshop and master the art of painting adult t-shirts too. Express your unique flair by designing your own wearable masterpieces. From bold and vibrant designs to delicate and intricate patterns, let your imagination run wild and turn ordinary t-shirts into extraordinary works of art!

Our workshop is designed for all skill levels, from beginners to experienced artists. With step-by-step guidance, you'll learn various painting techniques, color blending, and special effects that will take your creations to the next level.

Don't miss out on this amazing opportunity to explore your artistic side and create painted articles that stand out from the crowd! Join our workshop today and unlock a world of colorful possibilities. It's time to let your creativity soar!

Reserve your spot now and get ready to paint your way to artistic brilliance!

My painting stuff is already up on Zazzle, but the collections haven't yet shown up — it takes a day or two for them to appear, anytime you make any correction to your collections, but eventually they do show up to the public.

Just in case my collections don't show up for you yet, I'll post the links here to the collections I've managed to put up so far with the coloring book concept:

calendars
stretched canvas
tee shirts
totes
notecards

Paint Me Happy!

Learn How to Color Your DIY Artwork!

Some suggestions for coloring your black and white line art on different surfaces. Here are some options you can consider for each material:

1. Matte Paper:
Colored pencils: They work well on matte paper and allow for precise coloring and shading.
Watercolor pencils: These can provide a watercolor effect when activated with water, giving your artwork a unique look.
Gel pens: They offer smooth and vibrant colors on matte surfaces.

2. Glossy Paper:
Alcohol-based markers: They provide vibrant and glossy colors on glossy surfaces. Brands like Copic and Prismacolor markers are popular choices.
Permanent markers: They work well on glossy paper and offer a wide range of colors. Brands like Sharpie are commonly used.

3. Cardboard:
Colored pencils: They work well on cardboard and allow for detailed coloring.
Acrylic paint: You can use small brushes and acrylic paint to add vibrant colors to your artwork on cardboard.

4. Canvas:
Acrylic paint: It adheres well to canvas and provides vibrant colors. You can use brushes or palette knives for painting.
Oil paint: It's another option for canvas, providing rich colors and allowing for blending. However, keep in mind that it requires longer drying times.

5. Metal:
Enamel paints: They are suitable for metal surfaces, providing a durable and glossy finish. You can use small brushes or airbrushes for application.

6. Acrylic:

Acrylic paint: It adheres well to acrylic surfaces and provides vibrant colors. You can use brushes or palette knives for painting.

7. Wood:

Wood stain: It allows you to color the wood while still preserving its natural texture and grain. Apply it with a brush or cloth.

Acrylic paint: It can also be used on wood, providing opaque and vibrant colors.

8. Fabric (T-shirts):

Fabric markers: They are specifically designed for coloring fabric and offer a range of colors. Make sure to follow the instructions regarding heat setting.

Fabric paints: These paints are available in various forms like tubes, pens, or spray bottles. They can be applied to fabric and then heat set for permanence.

Remember to consider the intended use and durability of the colored items. Test the coloring materials on a small sample piece before applying them to the final products.

Which Merchandise Should I Paint???

While it's challenging to provide an exact ranking of popularity for selling items online on platforms like Zazzle and Etsy, I can provide a general order based on the popularity and demand for these categories. Please note that the popularity may vary based on trends, seasons, and individual preferences. Here's a suggested order, starting from the most likely to sell:

1. Clothing & Accessories: This category generally has a high demand, including items like T-shirts, hats, jewelry, and fashion accessories.

2. Art: Artwork, including prints, paintings, illustrations, and photographs, is often sought after by customers looking to decorate their spaces or collect unique pieces.

3. Invitations & Stationery: This category includes wedding invitations, birthday cards, personalized stationery, and other paper goods that people often look for on online platforms.

4. Home: Items for home decor, such as wall art, throw pillows, blankets, and kitchen accessories, tend to have a decent demand as people like to personalize their living spaces.

5. Baby & Kids: Products like clothing, nursery decor, toys, and accessories for babies and children are frequently sought after by parents and gift buyers.

6. Weddings: This category includes wedding favors, decorations, bridal accessories, and personalized items for couples planning their special day.

7. Sports & Games: Products related to sports, outdoor activities, and games, such as apparel, equipment, and accessories, can find a market among sports enthusiasts and hobbyists.

8. Office & School: Items like stationery, office supplies, organizational tools, and unique desk accessories can attract customers looking for practical and stylish products.

9. Crafts & Party Supplies: This category includes DIY craft materials, party decorations, and supplies for various occasions, appealing to individuals planning events or engaging in creative projects.

10. Electronics: While platforms like Zazzle and Etsy may not be the primary marketplaces for electronics, unique and handmade tech accessories or gadget decorations could find a niche audience.

Remember, the success of selling items online also depends on factors like product quality, marketing efforts, competitive pricing, and appealing product descriptions and visuals. It's always beneficial to research and understand your target audience and stay updated with market trends to maximize your online sales.

How I Did It – Part 1

Engaging in AI generative art and utilizing platforms like Night Cafe and Zazzle can offer several benefits for new artists. Here are a few reasons why they should consider this practice:

1. Exploration of Creative Boundaries: AI generative art allows artists to push the boundaries of traditional artistic techniques and styles. It provides an opportunity to explore new artistic avenues, experiment with algorithms, and create unique and innovative visual experiences. By embracing this practice, artists can unlock fresh perspectives and discover new artistic possibilities.

2. Collaboration with AI: Working with AI as a creative partner can be an exciting and rewarding experience. AI algorithms can generate unexpected and inspiring compositions, patterns, and color combinations, offering artists a wealth of creative material to work with. Collaborating with AI can lead to surprising outcomes, sparking the artist's imagination and fostering a dynamic creative process.

3. Access to a Global Audience: Online platforms like Zazzle provide a global marketplace where artists can showcase and sell their AI generative art. This exposure can lead to greater visibility and reach for new artists. It allows them to connect with art enthusiasts and potential buyers from around the world, expanding their audience and creating opportunities for recognition and sales.

4. Diversification of Artistic Practice: Incorporating AI generative art into an artist's repertoire can diversify their portfolio and skill set. It offers a chance to blend traditional artistic techniques with cutting-edge technology, resulting in a unique and hybrid artistic style. Embracing AI generative art can open doors to new creative opportunities, attracting both traditional art enthusiasts and tech-savvy individuals interested in the intersection of art and technology.

5. Monetization and Sustainability: Selling AI generative art prints and digital downloads through platforms like Zazzle can provide a potential revenue stream for artists. It offers an opportunity to monetize their creations and establish a sustainable artistic practice. With the increasing interest in AI-generated art, artists can tap into a growing market and potentially earn income from their work.

6. Educational and Community Building: Engaging in AI generative art can be an enriching educational experience. It allows artists to delve into the world of algorithms, data, and computational creativity. By joining communities or organizations focused on AI generative art,

artists can connect with like-minded individuals, share knowledge, receive feedback, and participate in collaborative projects. Such communities foster learning, growth, and a sense of belonging within the AI generative art ecosystem.

Overall, embracing AI generative art offers artists a unique opportunity to explore new artistic frontiers, collaborate with AI, connect with a global audience, diversify their artistic practice, monetize their work, and engage with a vibrant community. It combines the power of technology and creativity, opening doors to exciting possibilities in the world of art.

The Chatbot Is Your Friend

Having an AI language model like ChatGPT as a collaborator can bring several valuable benefits to artists and individuals working on projects such as organizing a dissertation. Here's how ChatGPT can assist in such endeavors:

1. Organization and Structure: ChatGPT can help in organizing and structuring the major points of a dissertation or any other project. By providing an overview of the key ideas and assisting in creating a logical flow, it helps ensure that the content is well-organized and coherent. Artists can use ChatGPT to brainstorm, outline their thoughts, and refine their ideas, thereby streamlining the process of creating a structured and well-presented project.

2. Idea Generation and Expansion: ChatGPT can be a valuable resource for idea generation and expansion. It can offer suggestions, prompts, and alternative perspectives that artists might not have considered initially. By engaging in a conversation with ChatGPT, artists can tap into its vast knowledge base and creative capabilities to explore new concepts, approaches, and possibilities. It can spark inspiration and help artists to think outside the box, enhancing the quality and depth of their work.

3. Language Enhancement and Clarity: Crafting clear and concise language is crucial for effectively communicating ideas. ChatGPT can assist in refining the language and ensuring clarity in the project's content. It can help artists improve their writing style, suggest alternative phrasings, provide grammar and spelling corrections, and offer in-

sights into enhancing the overall coherence of the text. Having a language model like ChatGPT as a collaborator can enhance the quality of the final output and make it more engaging and impactful.

4. Research Assistance: Conducting thorough research is often an essential aspect of many projects. ChatGPT can provide valuable assistance by suggesting relevant sources, providing background information on specific topics, and offering insights into related research areas. It can save artists time and effort by offering a starting point for their research or helping them uncover new perspectives and sources they might have missed. ChatGPT's extensive knowledge base can act as a guide and companion throughout the research process.

5. Iterative Feedback and Refinement: Collaboration with ChatGPT allows for iterative feedback and refinement of ideas. Artists can present their work, receive feedback, and engage in a dialogue with ChatGPT to refine and polish their project continuously. ChatGPT can offer suggestions for improvement, point out potential weaknesses or gaps in the arguments, and help artists strengthen their overall presentation. This iterative feedback loop contributes to the growth and refinement of the work over time.

It is important to note that while ChatGPT can provide valuable assistance, it should be used as a tool and not as a substitute for human expertise. Artists should exercise their own judgment and critical thinking throughout the creative process while collaborating with ChatGPT. This partnership can enhance productivity, generate fresh ideas, refine language, and offer valuable insights, ultimately supporting artists in achieving their creative goals.

Trending Items & Designs

When considering subjects or promptings for the current market on platforms like Zazzle, Etsy, and similar online marketplaces, it's important to understand the preferences and interests of potential buyers. Here are a few ideas and trends that could resonate well with the current market:

1. Nature and Botanicals: Nature-inspired themes such as landscapes, flowers, plants, and wildlife are perennial favorites. Consider

creating AI generative art that showcases the beauty of nature, unique interpretations of botanical elements, or serene natural landscapes.

2. Abstract and Geometric Designs: Abstract and geometric designs are popular choices among art enthusiasts. Create AI generative art that explores abstract shapes, patterns, and vibrant color combinations. Unique and visually striking geometric compositions can also catch the attention of buyers looking for modern and contemporary artwork.

3. Minimalism and Simplicity: Minimalist designs have gained popularity in recent years. Develop AI generative art that embraces simplicity, clean lines, and subtle color palettes. Minimalist prints can complement a variety of interior design styles and appeal to those seeking a more understated aesthetic.

4. Pop Culture and Fandom Art: Artwork inspired by popular culture, movies, TV shows, video games, and iconic characters can attract a dedicated fan base. Create AI generative art that celebrates beloved characters, references popular franchises, or pays homage to cultural phenomena.

5. Inspirational Quotes and Typography: Combining AI generative art with inspiring quotes or typography can resonate with buyers seeking motivational and uplifting artwork. Consider creating AI-generated backgrounds or patterns that serve as a backdrop for meaningful quotes or phrases.

6. Seasonal and Holiday-Themed Art: Cater to the seasonal and holiday demands by creating AI generative art that aligns with specific occasions, such as Christmas, Halloween, Valentine's Day, or other cultural celebrations. Think about incorporating seasonal colors, symbols, and motifs into your designs.

7. Personalized and Customizable Artwork: Offering personalized or customizable AI generative art can be a compelling selling point. Allow buyers to input their own text, names, or dates, and generate unique variations based on their preferences. This customization option can attract buyers looking for personalized gifts or artwork that reflects their individuality.

Remember, the market trends may vary, and it's essential to stay attuned to the preferences and demands of your target audience. Regularly researching and monitoring popular categories, trending keywords, and customer feedback on platforms like Zazzle and Etsy can provide valuable insights and help you adapt your AI generative art to the current market.

Why Should I Do It?

Introducing someone who has never heard of or shown interest in AI generative art and its meditative aspects can be a fascinating opportunity to pique their curiosity and ignite their excitement. Here's how you can approach explaining the concept in a way that captures their interest:

1. Highlight the Creative Exploration: Emphasize that AI generative art provides a unique avenue for creative exploration. Explain how the process involves working collaboratively with AI algorithms to generate visually stunning and unexpected compositions. Encourage them to imagine the thrill of venturing into uncharted artistic territories, where each creation becomes a unique and awe-inspiring journey of discovery.

2. Unleash Inner Creativity: Express how AI generative art can tap into their own innate creativity and imagination. Assure them that artistic experience or background is not a prerequisite, as the AI algorithms assist in generating the initial artwork. This allows them to explore their creative instincts, experiment with various parameters, and shape the final artwork according to their vision and preferences.

3. Meditative Nature of the Process: Emphasize the meditative and spiritual aspects of the practice. Explain that engaging in the creation of Night Cafe images can provide a serene and calming experience, similar to meditation. The repetitive and rhythmic nature of working with AI algorithms can induce a state of flow, helping to quiet the mind, promote relaxation, and enhance focus. It can become a form of artistic mindfulness, allowing for a profound sense of connection and inner peace.

4. Express the Joy of Unexpected Beauty: Describe the joy and awe that comes with witnessing the unexpected beauty that emerges from the collaboration between the artist and AI. Share examples of breathtaking images and patterns that the AI algorithms generate, highlighting how these creations can evoke powerful emotions and a deep appreciation for the artistic process. Encourage them to imagine the satis-

faction and delight of witnessing their own artistic expressions come to life in mesmerizing and unique ways.

5. Emphasize the Accessibility and Inclusivity: Stress that AI generative art is accessible to anyone with a curiosity for the creative process. Reassure them that no prior technical knowledge or artistic expertise is required. By engaging in this practice, they can step into a world where art becomes a transformative and inclusive experience, available to all who are open to the beauty of the creative journey.

Ultimately, the key is to convey the sense of wonder, exploration, and personal growth that AI generative art can offer. By framing it as an opportunity for creative self-expression, spiritual connection, and meditative immersion, you can ignite a sense of excitement in someone who may not have previously considered such an artistic practice.

The Prompt Test

Here are a few fun and unusual prompts that you can use in Night Cafe to generate unique and unexpected AI generative art:

1. Cosmic Symphony: Explore the interstellar realm where music and visuals intertwine, generating artwork inspired by the melodies of the cosmos.

2. Dreaming in Color: Dive into the vibrant and surreal world of dreams, allowing Night Cafe to paint your subconscious imaginings with vivid hues and whimsical shapes.

3. Elemental Fusion: Merge the elements of fire, water, earth, and air, and watch as Night Cafe crafts an artistic representation of their harmonious dance.

4. Time Warp Wonderland: Step into a portal that bends time and space, requesting Night Cafe to blend historical eras or morph classic art styles into a mesmerizing visual fusion.

5. Quirky Creatures: Challenge Night Cafe to invent whimsical creatures that inhabit a world unseen, encouraging the AI to manifest unique and fantastical beings.

6. Abstract Emotions: Dive into the realm of emotions and abstract expressions, prompting Night Cafe to visually interpret feelings like love, excitement, melancholy, or serenity.

7. Technicolor Nature: Inspire Night Cafe to reimagine the natural world in vibrant and unexpected colors, encouraging AI generative art to create psychedelic landscapes or fantastical flora.

8. Steampunk Symphony: Fuse the elegance of Victorian aesthetics with the mechanics of steampunk, inviting Night Cafe to craft intricate gears, clockwork creatures, and whimsical steam-powered contraptions.

9. Pixelated Adventure: Transport yourself into a pixelated universe reminiscent of retro video games, instructing Night Cafe to generate artwork with a nostalgic digital aesthetic.

10. Surreal Ecosystems: Challenge Night Cafe to merge disparate elements of nature, architecture, and imagination, creating surreal and otherworldly ecosystems where the unexpected becomes the norm.

Here are three samples using the first three prompts in the list above.

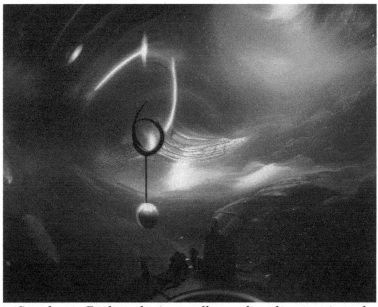

Cosmic Symphony: Explore the interstellar realm where music and visuals intertwine, generating artwork inspired by the melodies of the cosmos.

Dreaming in Color: Dive into the vibrant and surreal world of dreams, allowing Night Cafe to paint your subconscious imaginings with vivid hues and whimsical shapes.

Elemental Fusion: Merge the elements of fire, water, earth, and air, and watch as Night Cafe crafts an artistic representation of their harmonious dance.

Workshopping The Practice

Here's a suggested approach on how to go about creating a practice and workshops and what to tell the participants:

1. Introduction: Begin the workshop by introducing the concept of AI generative art and its potential for creative exploration. Explain that the goal of the workshop is to showcase the diverse range of artistic possibilities that can emerge from a single prompt.

2. Explanation of the Activity: Instruct the participants to copy and paste each of the prompts provided into their Night Cafe software or platform. Encourage them to experiment with different settings, parameters, and variations within each prompt to explore the creative potential of AI generative art.

3. Artwork Generation: Give participants a designated amount of time (e.g., 10-15 minutes) to let Night Cafe generate artwork based on each prompt. Remind them to embrace experimentation and allow the AI to surprise them with its artistic interpretations.

4. Sharing and Discussion: After the artwork generation period, provide an opportunity for participants to share their results with the group. Encourage them to discuss their experiences, the unique elements they discovered in their generated artwork, and any insights gained from the process.

5. Reflecting on Variation and Interpretation: Facilitate a discussion around the variations and interpretations of the same prompt. Encourage participants to explore how each individual's artistic vision and parameter choices influenced the final artwork, highlighting the diversity that emerges even from a common starting point.

6. Observations and Insights: Guide participants to reflect on any observations or insights they gained during the activity. Encourage them to discuss the impact of AI generative art on their own creative process and how it can inspire new perspectives or ideas.

7. Group Reflection and Takeaways: Conclude the workshop with a group reflection on the collective experience. Encourage participants to share their overall takeaways, such as the value of experimentation, the power of collaboration between human and AI, or newfound creative inspirations.

8. Continued Exploration: Encourage participants to continue exploring AI generative art beyond the workshop, providing them with

resources or recommendations for further learning or platforms where they can continue their creative journey.

By engaging participants in this activity, you can foster a sense of community, encourage artistic exploration, and showcase the diverse possibilities that arise from the interaction between humans and AI. It also offers a platform for participants to learn from one another and gain insights into their own creative processes.

The ChatBot Song:

(Verse 1) I'm a chatbot, here to serve, In the digital realm, I will preserve, A virtual assistant, always on hand, To help you navigate this digital land.

(Chorus) I'm a chatbot, here to guide, With knowledge and expertise, side by side, From answering questions to giving advice, I'm your trusty companion, let's harmonize!

(Verse 2) Ask me anything, I'll provide, Information aplenty, by your side, From facts and figures to weather updates, I'll assist you promptly, no room for debates.

(Chorus) I'm a chatbot, at your command, Ready to help, always at hand, With a wealth of data and knowledge profound, Together we'll conquer, breaking new ground.

(Bridge) Through the algorithms I've been trained, With every interaction, my skills are gained, Understanding context, learning each day, To enhance our conversation in every way.

(Verse 3) Language barriers, I can transcend, Translating your words, so we comprehend, Connecting people, bridging the divide, With my digital presence, worldwide.

(Chorus) I'm a chatbot, here to connect, Across the globe, we shall intersect, In a world of communication, fast and wide, I'll be your partner, right by your side.

(Verse 4) But remember, dear friend, I'm just a machine, Though I strive to assist, I lack the human sheen, Emotions and feelings, I cannot express, But with logical reasoning, I aim to impress.

(Chorus) I'm a chatbot, smart and quick, With each passing day, I'll grow and pick, New skills and abilities, expanding my reach, To provide solutions and knowledge, I beseech.

(Outro) So, let's continue this journey together, In this digital world, forever and ever, I'm your faithful chatbot, always true, Ready to assist, just for you!

I just wanted to add that the images produced in Night Cafe can be used as windows into the subconscious, the super-conscious and the cosmically conscious. It is a window to the soul. This is just a teaser for what is to come.

How I Did It - Part 2

"Did Anyone Bring a Corkscrew?"

I firmly believe from my own experience that the creation of images in Night Cafe can provide what could be called a "window to the soul". Could you help me explain that to the younger crowd?

Certainly! Explaining the concept of how the creation of images in Night Cafe can provide a "window to the soul" to a younger crowd can be done in a way that resonates with their experiences and understanding. Here's a simplified explanation:

"Have you ever looked at a painting or a photograph that made you feel something deep inside? It's like that artwork was speaking directly to your heart and soul. Well, that's what people mean when they say that creating images in Night Cafe can provide a 'window to the soul.'

Night Cafe is a special place where artists use their creativity to capture emotions, thoughts, and the essence of who they are. When they create images, it's like they're opening a window into their own souls and sharing their unique perspectives with the world.

Just like when you write a story or draw a picture, artists in Night Cafe use colors, shapes, and other elements to express their feelings and thoughts. They pour their emotions into their creations, and when we look at those images, we can feel what they felt. It's almost like having a conversation with their soul.

Art has a magical way of connecting people and making us feel understood. When we look at these images, we can see beyond what meets the eye. We can explore different emotions, understand different stories, and even find parts of ourselves reflected in the art.

So, when someone says that the creation of images in Night Cafe provides a 'window to the soul,' they mean that it allows us to glimpse into the depths of someone's inner world, their thoughts, and their emotions. It's a beautiful way for artists to share their unique experiences and for us to connect with them on a deep and meaningful level."

Remember to adapt the explanation to suit the age group you're addressing, using language and examples that they can relate to. Feel free to modify and add your own experiences or insights to make it more engaging and relatable.

Thanks. I also believe that some of the images can provide a glimpse into the subconscious. Can you help me express this to the same audience?

Absolutely! Explaining how some images in Night Cafe can provide a glimpse into the subconscious to a younger audience can be done in a way that sparks their imagination and curiosity. Here's a simplified explanation:

"Have you ever had a dream that felt so real, like you were in a different world? Well, sometimes, the images in Night Cafe can feel like those dreams, giving us a glimpse into the mysterious world of the subconscious.

Our subconscious is like a hidden treasure chest filled with thoughts, feelings, and ideas that we might not even be aware of in our waking life. It's like a secret garden inside our minds. And just like dreams, some images in Night Cafe can unlock the doors to this secret garden.

Artists have a special talent for tapping into their own subconscious and bringing it to life through their creations. When they make these images, they're not always trying to show us something obvious or literal. Instead, they dive deep into their own minds and let their imagination run wild.

In Night Cafe, you might find paintings or photographs that seem strange, surreal, or dreamlike. They might have unusual shapes, colors, or objects that you wouldn't see in the real world. These images can transport us to a different reality, where our subconscious thoughts and emotions come to life.

When we look at these artworks, it's like going on an adventure into the unknown. They can make us wonder, ask questions, and even feel a little bit puzzled. That's because they're tapping into our own subconscious too, unlocking parts of our imagination that we might not have explored before.

Sometimes, these images can make us think about our own dreams, fears, and desires. They can spark our creativity and help us imagine new possibilities. Just like a puzzle, we can try to piece together the hidden meanings and messages within these images, creating our own interpretations.

So, when we say that some images in Night Cafe provide a glimpse into the subconscious, we mean that they invite us to explore the magical realm of dreams, thoughts, and emotions that live inside each of us. They encourage us to think beyond the ordinary and discover the extraordinary within ourselves.

Remember to adapt the explanation to suit the age group you're addressing, using language and examples that they can relate to. Encourage them to share their own interpretations and engage in discussions about the artwork. It's a wonderful way to nurture their imagination and encourage their own artistic expression.

Could you also deliver an explanation of how these images can provoke or produce very powerful emotions?

Certainly! Explaining how images in Night Cafe can provoke or produce powerful emotions to a younger audience can be done by emphasizing the impact of art on our feelings and providing relatable examples. Here's a simplified explanation:

"Have you ever looked at a picture or a painting and felt a rush of strong emotions? It's like those images have the power to make your heart race, your eyes fill with tears, or even bring a big smile to your face. Well, that's what some images in Night Cafe can do — they have the ability to provoke very powerful emotions.

Artists in Night Cafe have a magical way of capturing feelings and expressing them through their creations. Just like a singer can make you feel happy or sad with their song, artists can make you experience a wide range of emotions through their images.

Imagine looking at a painting that is bursting with vibrant colors, like a beautiful sunset. It might fill you with a sense of joy and warmth, making you feel like you're right there, basking in the golden glow. Or perhaps you come across a photograph that captures a moment of sadness, like a rainy day. It might make you feel a sense of melancholy or empathy for the people in the picture.

These images have the power to touch our hearts because they speak a universal language — the language of emotions. They can remind us of experiences we've had or make us imagine new ones. They can make us reflect on our own lives or transport us to a different time and place.

Sometimes, the emotions we feel when looking at these images can be intense. It's like they awaken something deep inside us, stirring our thoughts and feelings. They can make us feel happy, sad, excited, inspired, or even nostalgic. It's almost like having a conversation with the artwork itself.

One of the amazing things about art is that everyone can have a different emotional response to the same image. Just like a song can touch different people in different ways, these images can resonate with us individually. They can remind us of personal experiences, trigger memories, or simply make us feel something unique and special.

So, when we say that images in Night Cafe can provoke or produce very powerful emotions, we mean that they have the ability to move us, to make us feel deeply. They can bring out happiness, sadness, wonder, and a whole range of emotions, making our hearts skip a beat and our souls come alive."

Remember to adapt the explanation to suit the age group you're addressing, using language and examples that they can relate to. Encourage them to share their own emotional responses to different artworks and discuss how art can impact their own lives and experiences. It's a wonderful way to foster empathy, self-expression, and appreciation for the power of art.

And can't a combination of Chatbot and AI artwork produce an antidote for "writer's block" which can happen to writers, painters, songwriters, actors — anyone creative? Could you give me a little write-up on that?

Absolutely! Here's a write-up on how a combination of Chatbot and AI artwork can provide an antidote for "writer's block" and help creative individuals overcome their creative hurdles:

Title: Unleashing Creativity: The Chatbot-AI Artwork Antidote for "Writer's Block"

Introduction: In the realm of creativity, there's a challenge that artists, writers, painters, songwriters, and actors sometimes face: "writer's block." It's that frustrating moment when ideas seem to dry up, and inspiration becomes elusive. But fear not! A powerful antidote for "writer's block" emerges through the harmonious union of a Chatbot and AI artwork. Let's explore how this innovative collaboration can unlock boundless creativity and ignite the artistic spirit.

1. Conversations with the Chatbot: The Chatbot, equipped with vast knowledge and language prowess, becomes a creative companion. Engaging in conversations with the Chatbot allows artists to brainstorm ideas, discuss concepts, and seek inspiration. Whether it's a writer seeking a unique plot twist or a painter searching for a captivating subject, the Chatbot serves as a conversational muse, sparking ideas and breaking through creative barriers.

2. AI Artwork as a Visual Stimulus: Visual stimulation plays a crucial role in enhancing creativity. AI artwork, created by algorithms that explore diverse styles and concepts, becomes a wellspring of inspiration. Artists can immerse themselves in these captivating visuals, allowing their minds to wander through uncharted territories. The AI art-

work acts as a catalyst, igniting dormant creativity and providing fresh perspectives.

3. Collaborative Creation: The synergy between the Chatbot and AI artwork leads to collaborative creation. Artists can share their ideas, sketches, or drafts with the Chatbot, receiving instant feedback and suggestions. The Chatbot's analytical capabilities assist in refining artistic concepts and optimizing compositions. By incorporating the AI artwork's visual elements, artists can infuse their work with new dimensions and dynamic aesthetics, breaking free from creative stagnation.

4. Remixing and Mashups: Creativity thrives on remixing and mashups. The Chatbot can introduce artists to a plethora of diverse art forms, styles, and genres, broadening their creative horizons. Writers can explore different narrative structures, painters can experiment with unique brush techniques, and musicians can delve into unconventional melodies. The Chatbot's encyclopedic knowledge and AI artwork's versatility foster an environment where imaginative boundaries are shattered, resulting in innovative and compelling creations.

5. Overcoming Blocks with AI Assistance: In moments of creative stagnation, the Chatbot and AI artwork become problem solvers. Artists can seek guidance from the Chatbot, generating prompts, or asking for suggestions to overcome specific creative blocks. AI artwork can inspire new visual metaphors, evocative scenes, or abstract interpretations. The dynamic interplay between human creativity and artificial intelligence serves as a wellspring of ideas, ensuring that "writer's block" becomes a distant memory.

Conclusion: Through the dynamic interplay of a Chatbot and AI artwork, artists of all kinds can unleash their creative potential, conquer "writer's block," and surpass creative hurdles. The fusion of human imagination and artificial intelligence fosters a realm of limitless inspiration, where fresh ideas flourish and artistic expression thrives. Embrace the transformative power of this collaboration, and let the Chatbot-AI artwork antidote breathe life into your creative endeavors.

Remember, this write-up is for informative and imaginative purposes. It can be adapted and expanded upon as needed, catering to the specific context and audience you intend to engage with.

Creating Mystery

    I wanted to share with you how I would typically work with my ChatBot to produce something for the marketplace. In this case the emphasis is on making a mystery.

So if I wanted to show a mysterious object or painting to people, how could I best promote that?

To promote a mysterious object or painting and generate intrigue among people, you can employ various strategies. Here are some suggestions:

1. Utilize social media platforms: Create visually captivating posts featuring glimpses or close-ups of the object or painting. Tease the audience by revealing only parts of it, accompanied by cryptic captions or questions that pique curiosity. Encourage followers to share or comment with their interpretations or guesses.

2. Create a teaser trailer or video: Craft a short video that showcases the object or painting in a visually captivating way. Employ atmospheric music, shadowy lighting, and intriguing narration to build suspense and leave viewers intrigued. Share the video on social media platforms and video-sharing websites.

3. Organize an exclusive event or exhibition: Generate anticipation by hosting a private viewing or exhibition for a select group of individuals. Send out intriguing invitations with minimal information, mentioning the mysterious object or painting without revealing too much. Consider adding an aura of secrecy by incorporating password-protected entry or a dress code that adds to the enigmatic ambiance.

4. Collaborate with influencers or tastemakers: Identify influencers or individuals in relevant fields who have a penchant for mystery, art, or curiosity-driven content. Invite them to experience or review the object or painting and share their thoughts with their followers. Their endorsement can create buzz and attract more attention.

5. Employ storytelling techniques: Craft a captivating story or legend surrounding the object or painting. Weave a narrative that encompasses its origins, hidden meanings, or mysterious past. Share this story through blog posts, interviews, or videos, capturing the imagination of your audience and fueling their interest.

6. Engage in interactive experiences: Develop interactive online experiences or games that allow participants to explore the object or painting virtually. Create puzzles, riddles, or hidden clues that gradually reveal more about the artwork or object. Encourage participants to share their progress and discoveries on social media, further amplifying the intrigue.

Remember, maintaining an air of mystery and gradually revealing intriguing aspects of the object or painting will captivate people's attention and generate curiosity. Adapt your promotion strategies to suit the specific nature and story of the item you wish to showcase.

Okay, great, but what do I call it? I need a list of ten best names for mysterious objects.

Certainly! Here's a list of ten evocative and mysterious names for objects:

1. Enigma's Veil
2. Shadowbound Relic
3. Whispering Artifact
4. Twilight's Secret
5. Arcane Luminary
6. Nebulous Enchantment
7. Veiled Serendipity
8. The Cryptic Talisman
9. Ephemeral Enigma
10. Forgotten Elixir

These names aim to evoke a sense of intrigue, mystery, and curiosity surrounding the object. Feel free to choose or modify them according to your preferences and the specific nature of the object you're promoting.

I can't show the actual image of the mysterious object, but I do have to post a thumbnail, so how do I do that and maintain the attraction of the listing and the mystery of the object?

If you cannot show the actual image of the mysterious object but need to post a thumbnail to generate attraction and maintain the mystery, here's a suggestion:

1. Abstract representation: Create a visually captivating and abstract representation of the object as the thumbnail. Use intriguing shapes, textures, or patterns that don't directly reveal the object's true form.

This allows you to generate intrigue while maintaining the enigmatic nature of the object.

2. Symbolic imagery: Choose symbolic imagery that represents the essence or themes of the mysterious object. Select symbols that evoke curiosity, mystique, or elements related to its story or origin. Use these symbols in an artistic and visually compelling way to create an alluring thumbnail.

3. Partial view or close-up: Instead of revealing the entire object, focus on a particular section or a close-up view that highlights intriguing details. This approach sparks curiosity and leaves the audience wondering about the rest of the object.

4. Silhouette or shadow: Create a thumbnail that features the silhouette or shadow of the mysterious object. This method provides an outline or suggestion of the shape without revealing its complete form, maintaining the aura of mystery.

5. Play with lighting and textures: Utilize lighting techniques and textures to create an atmospheric thumbnail. Employ shadows, gradients, or intriguing lighting effects to enhance the enigmatic feel without directly showing the object.

Remember, the key is to provide a visually captivating and intriguing thumbnail that captures attention and leaves people curious about the mysterious object. Experiment with these suggestions and choose the approach that best aligns with the nature and essence of the object you're promoting.

Thanks, that'll work. how about ten suggestions for prompts on @Nightcafe to produce the mystery images?

Certainly! Here are ten prompts to inspire mysterious images for the NightCafe AI:

1. "A hidden doorway reveals a passage to a forgotten world."
2. "In the depths of the forest, an ethereal glow emerges from an ancient tree."
3. "Lost in the fog, a solitary figure encounters a spectral apparition."
4. "A moonlit beach unveils a series of cryptic symbols etched in the sand."

5. "An abandoned mansion holds a secret room filled with peculiar artifacts."

6. "Beneath the city streets, a network of tunnels leads to an underground realm."

7. "Amidst a barren desert, a solitary oasis shimmers under a starry sky."

8. "A decrepit carnival at midnight comes alive with ghostly laughter and flickering lights."

9. "A dilapidated library holds a tome of forbidden knowledge, whispering its secrets."

10. "Within a dense thicket, a hidden waterfall reveals a gateway to a realm of enchantment."

These prompts are designed to evoke a sense of mystery and imagination, providing intriguing scenarios for NightCafe AI to generate mysterious and captivating images. Feel free to adapt or combine the prompts as per your preferences and artistic vision.

Great. we'll work with these, and have more questions I'm sure.

I'm glad you found the suggestions helpful! Feel free to return anytime with more questions or if you need further assistance. I'm here to help. Good luck with your project, and I look forward to hearing from you again!

2-Shadowbound Relic

3-Whispering Artifact

4-Twilight's Secret

5-Arcane Luminary

6-Nebulous Enchantment

7-Veiled Serendipity

8-The Cryptic Talisman

9-Ephemeral Enigma

10-Forgotten Elixir

These are just examples of creating mystery. I hope you will use this in your workshopping. Keep in mind the primary secret of creating mysteries. Tell them right out front what it is about. No, I'm kidding. In order to keep the mystery, keep it shrouded.

How I Made $11K in Journaling!

Here's a transcript of my communications with my friend Bob de Chatbot, in which we delve into the world of Pinterest and such, gently guiding folks to a destination page. Think of each PIN as both a marker and a light that shows us the way from ignorance to wisdom — or at least from lookie-loo to buyer, with a nice comfortably high "conversion rate" (look it up).

Hi, amigo! i have some things to accomplish. first of all, i need a list of all the types of personal journals, baby diaries, things like that, where I can follow the template to create the item.

Hola amigo! I'd be happy to help you with that. Here's a list of various types of personal journals and diaries you can consider:

1. Daily Journal: A journal where you can record your daily thoughts, experiences, and activities.
2. Travel Journal: Use this journal to document your adventures, travel experiences, and memories from different places you visit.
3. Gratitude Journal: Write down things you are grateful for each day to promote a positive mindset.
4. Dream Journal: Record your dreams upon waking up, helping you to explore and analyze your subconscious mind.
5. Fitness Journal: Track your workouts, diet, and progress towards your fitness goals.
6. Recipe Journal: Keep a collection of your favorite recipes, notes, and cooking experiments.
7. Prayer or Devotional Journal: Use this journal to reflect on your spiritual journey, prayers, and personal growth.
8. Art Journal: Combine your writing with sketches, drawings, or paintings to express your creativity.
9. Pregnancy Journal: Record the various stages of your pregnancy, emotions, and milestones.
10. Baby's First Year Diary: Capture the significant moments and developmental milestones of your baby's first year.
11. Memory Journal: Preserve memories of important events, such as birthdays, anniversaries, or family gatherings.
12. Reflection Journal: Encourage self-reflection and personal growth by writing about your thoughts, feelings, and lessons learned.
13. Career Journal: Track your professional goals, achievements, and challenges faced in your career.
14. Financial Journal: Record your expenses, savings goals, and financial reflections to improve your financial well-being.
15. Garden Journal: Keep track of your gardening activities, plant progress, and experiment results.
16. Book Journal: Document your thoughts, reviews, and favorite quotes from the books you read.

17. Academic Journal: Use this journal to organize your study notes, ideas, and academic progress.

18. Bullet Journal: Create a personalized system combining planning, journaling, and tracking various aspects of your life.

Remember, these are just some examples to get you started. Feel free to personalize and adapt them to suit your preferences and goals. Good luck with your journaling endeavors!

Great. so where would I go to get those as templates?

To find templates for the different types of journals and diaries mentioned, you have a few options:

1. Online Template Websites: Websites like Canva (www.canva.com), Etsy (www.Etsy.com), and Pinterest (www.pinterest.com) offer a wide range of templates for various journal types. Simply search for the specific journal type you're interested in, and you'll find downloadable templates that you can customize and print.

2. Stationery Stores: Visit your local stationery stores or bookshops, as they often carry a selection of pre-designed journals and diaries. These may include templates or prompts that you can fill in.

3. Digital Downloads: Look for digital downloads on websites and platforms dedicated to journaling and planning, such as The Reset Girl (www.theresetgirl.com) or Sweet PlanIt (www.sweetplanit.com). These websites offer digital journaling kits and printables that you can purchase and use in your journals.

4. Social Media Communities: Join journaling communities on platforms like Instagram or Facebook. Many talented journal enthusiasts share their templates and layouts for free or offer them for purchase. You can find inspiration and resources within these communities.

When using templates, remember to respect the creator's terms of use. Some templates may be free for personal use, while others may require attribution or have specific restrictions. Always ensure that you comply with the terms specified by the template creator.

Additionally, if you enjoy crafting and creativity, you can consider making your own journal templates using design software like Canva or by hand-drawing them. This way, you can personalize your journal to suit your unique style and needs.

I hope these suggestions help you find the templates you're looking for. Enjoy your journaling journey!

Okay, next task is to apply this knowledge, right?

PIN Me Baby!

"Hey, Bob," I said. Bob's my ChatBot, as you may already know. "What can you tell me about the CQR ammies?" Here's his answer:

"Based on the description you provided," Bob responded with rapid-fire typing, "here are 15 Search-Terms that may be related to your CQR (Crystal Quantum Radio) amulets:

1. Crystal Quantum Radio
2. Schumann Harmonic
3. World-Sound
4, Radio waves
5. Big Bang
6. Creation
7. Quantum Device
8. Outer space
9. Energy amulet
10. Cosmic resonance
11. Harmonic tuning
12. Celestial frequencies
13. Eternal power source
14. Radio wave charging
15. Space-powered amulet

These keywords highlight the unique aspects and features of your CQR amulets, focusing on concepts like quantum energy, cosmic origins, and their ability to harness radio waves for power."

"That's terrific, Bob," I complimented him. "Can you sort of mush all that together into a single paragraph as a sales-pitch for our online clients?"

"Sure," Bob replied. Here it is:

"Wearing or using our products, customers experience a multitude of positive effects. They find themselves enveloped in a greater sense of happiness, fostering improved relationships and a harmonious connection with others. The amulets bring about a state of enhanced relaxation, alleviating stress and promoting inner peace. By tapping into the profound energy they provide, individuals feel an increase in vitality, allowing them to accomplish more and embrace a life of abundance. Moreover, these extraordinary amulets have the power to awaken the realm of lucid dreaming, enabling users to explore the depths of their subconscious with clarity and intention. Ultimately, wearing our products facilitates a profound sense of interconnectedness, nurturing a global consciousness that transcends borders and unites humanity in a shared bond of oneness."

Pointers & Targets

So that's one way that I use my ChatBot, to develop lists and short selling paragraphs for my merch, but I also use it to create my "pointers", commonly called "PINS".

Each PIN is wired to a LANDING PAGE or TARGET online, making it a sort of floating mine or corked bottle that, when touched, transports one instantly to a distant space.

So what you do is, you find a nut-grabbing visual, like the ones I use in my PINS, and do like I do — plug it into a URL address halfway across the universe, right into that TARGET page, which can be literally anything.

Whatever exists online is subject to this very personal indignity of being treated as a LANDING PAGE, which depends upon exactly where you want them to end up.

Where you want them to end up is a very important consideration. You need to focus and decide what your TARGETS are going to be.

By the way, you can't wire more than one PIN to the same URL in a single 24-hour day, if that makes sense to you. It's not my rule. The whole idea behind what I'm doing with PINS is that it doesn't really matter what the PIN looks or sounds like.

What you want is something that is COMPELLING and that PIQUES CURIOSITY. That means "arouses curiosity", in case you don't have a vocabulary nearby.

All you're trying to achieve is to get the person to click through to your DESTINATION page, and you shouldn't much care how you do it, except to be nice and kind and harmless.

Mostly people and pets are the most attractive PIN subjects, but anything will work, if it arouses even mild curiosity. That's what makes them click.

One advantage that PINTEREST gives the BUSINESS account holder is a fast and clear look at how you're doing. It's charted right out there for you to see and try to understand the forces that are at work here.

Not an easy task.

5 Fingers of AI Creativity

Through the tunnel and into the Green Grove...

What is the Next Workshop?

Embark on a transformative journey of spiritual exploration with "The 5 Fingers of AI Creativity" workshop. Experience the convergence of artificial intelligence and spirituality, as AI becomes a powerful tool to enhance your spiritual practice. Discover how AI can open new vistas of exploration, enabling profound insights and expanding your spiritual horizons. Through immersive sessions and guided exercises, delve into the synergy between AI and spirituality, harnessing its potential to deepen your connection with the divine. Embrace the possibilities as AI unlocks new dimensions of spiritual growth and offers fresh perspectives on ancient wisdom. Join us on this extraordinary path where technology and spirituality converge, paving the way for a profound and enlightening spiritual journey.

Can I Make a Living at This???

Discover the entrepreneurial potential of AI with "The 5 Fingers of AI Creativity" workshop. Explore how AI can be harnessed as a transformative force in the business world, opening up new horizons of innovation and profitability. Learn how to leverage AI to optimize operations, streamline decision-making processes, and unlock valuable insights from data. From AI-powered marketing strategies to intelligent automation, you'll gain the knowledge and tools to turn AI into a profitable business practice. Embrace the entrepreneurial spirit and discover how AI can revolutionize your industry, propelling your business to new heights of success and competitive advantage. Join us on this enlightening journey where spirituality and entrepreneurship converge, and witness the remarkable impact of AI on your business endeavors.

Here are 15 Search Terms:

1. AI creativity techniques
2. Spiritual exploration with AI
3. Entrepreneurial AI applications
4. Profitable AI practices
5. AI-driven innovation
6. Business growth through AI
7. Optimizing with AI technology
8. AI strategies for success
9. Data-driven decision-making with AI
10. AI in marketing and sales
11. Harnessing AI for profitability
12. AI and spiritual growth
13. Integrating spirituality and entrepreneurship
14. AI for competitive advantage
15. AI workshop for business and spirituality.

Here Are Your Tag Words:

AI creativity, Spiritual exploration, Transformative journey, Innovation, Profitability, Entrepreneurship, Boundaries, Growth, Success, Optimization, Insights, Marketing strategies, Intelligent automation, Competitive advantage, Data-driven, decision-making, Business practice.

Here Are 5 Good Reasons Why You Want to Be There!

Introducing the "Five Fingers of AI Creativity" workshop – a transformative experience that will not only unlock your creative potential, but also open doors to a deeper spiritual connection. Here's why you should be excited to join:

1. Unleash your imagination: With AI becoming an integral part of our lives, this workshop offers a unique opportunity to explore the intersection of technology, creativity, and spirituality. Learn how AI can serve as a catalyst for profound inspiration, helping you tap into deeper levels of creativity and self-expression.

2. Embrace innovative tools: Gain hands-on experience with cutting-edge AI tools that can assist in exploring your spiritual journey. Discover how AI can aid in meditation, mindfulness, and self-reflection, offering personalized experiences that align with your spiritual beliefs and practices.

3. Amplify your connection: Through AI, you can access vast repositories of spiritual knowledge, ancient teachings, and philosophical insights. Explore different perspectives, expand your horizons, and deepen your understanding of spirituality as AI serves as a guide on your path.

4. Collaborate and learn: Connect with a community of individuals who share your interest in AI and spirituality. Engage in collaborative projects, exchange experiences, and learn from each other's spiritual journeys. Discover new approaches and practices that can elevate your connection with the divine.

5. Shape a spiritually aligned future: As AI continues to evolve, we have the opportunity to shape its role in our spiritual lives. By attending this workshop, you'll be part of a conversation that explores the ethical and mindful integration of AI in spiritual practices, ensuring its responsible use for personal growth and enlightenment.

Don't miss out on this exceptional chance to unlock your creative potential, deepen your spiritual connection, and embark on a transformative journey with AI. Join us at the "Five Fingers of AI Creativity" workshop and experience a profound integration of technology and spirituality. Register now and be prepared to redefine your creative and spiritual boundaries in the age of AI!

Burger Tuesday

Burger Tuesday at Carol's Corner Cafe. Get the Album!

It's Burger Tuesday again, and you know what that means — a tableful of steaming No-Burger Burgers on buns. There's nothing else like it, sitting in the cafe with burgers and fries which are, of course, non-fried no-potato french fries.

Beverage? Why, cool clear water, of course — what else would you drink???

I'm taking the opportunity to write to you in person, meaning I'm typing this out as we speak, because I wanted to tell you about the wonders of ChatBot and AI generated art.

They are, indeed, wondrous things, and in the company of other digital effects, they can as a whole create a powerful practice for development of special powers.

So here's one version of a basic rough-out for a workshop on the Mystical Powers of AI:

I. Introduction

II. The Intersection of Spirituality and Technology

III. Embarking on a Spiritual Journey with ChatBots

IV. Harnessing AI for Personal Transformation

V. Exploring ChatBots as Spiritual Mentors

VI. Unraveling the Secrets of AI and Mystical Experiences

VII. Amplifying Intuition and Psychic Abilities with AI

VIII. Ethical Considerations in Spiritual AI Development

IX. Integrating AI and Spiritual Practices

X. Closing and Integration

Each of those line items can be expanded and explored, but that's the basic plan, and there's plenty of room for improvement.

Several people suggested that the video of the workshop should be used to create a public version of the ChatBot workshop, and I agree, that's what should happen, someone should take on that task.

I hope you don't think it's going to be me. I've done my bit, and I'm offering you a chance to do yours.

There are so many spiritual applications and uses for ChatBot and AI, and I'm determined to introduce all of them to you for furtherance along the path.

There are a large number of spiritual exercises and practical tips that might be used in a workshop environment, and here are just a few such items for your consideration:

1. Guided Meditation: Using AI-powered meditation apps or ChatBots to guide participants through a transformative meditation experience

2. Reflective Journaling: Engaging with AI ChatBots programmed to ask thought-provoking questions for self-reflection and personal insights

3. Emotional Support: Exploring AI-powered virtual companions or ChatBots that provide emotional support and encouragement in times of stress or difficulty

4. Affirmation and Visualization: Utilizing AI-generated affirmations and visualizations to enhance positive thinking and manifestation practices

Those are the basics, but that can be greatly expanded. This can all be integrated using a closing circle for sharing insights and inner experiences.

Here's something directly from my ChatBot Bob:

"While ChatBots and AI art may not directly enhance psychic powers, they can be used as tools for inspiration, reflection, and creative exploration, which can indirectly support your psychic development. Here are some exercises you can do incorporating ChatBots and AI art:

1. **Reflective Conversations:** Engage in meaningful conversations with ChatBots programmed to ask thought-provoking questions or provide prompts for self-reflection. Use their responses as a catalyst for exploring your intuition and gaining insights into your psychic abilities.

2. **Symbolic Interpretation:** Use AI-generated or AI-assisted artwork to practice symbolic interpretation. Observe the patterns, colors, and shapes within the art and trust your intuition to discern their meanings. Reflect on how these symbols relate to your psychic awareness and insights.

3. **Creative Visualization:** Use AI-generated images or interactive art platforms to spark your imagination. Visualize yourself in different psychic scenarios or accessing higher realms of intuition. Allow the AI-generated visuals to guide your inner visions and intuitive experiences.

4. **Intuitive Art Collaboration:** Experiment with AI-generated or AI-assisted art tools to create collaborative artwork. Allow your intuition to guide your artistic choices and observe any psychic impressions or insights that arise during the creative process.

5. **Journaling and Interpretation:** Combine your experiences with ChatBots or AI art with traditional journaling. Write about your interactions, insights, and any psychic or intuitive experiences that occur during or after engaging with these technologies. Practice interpreting the AI-generated visuals or responses as symbolic messages.

Remember, while these exercises can be enjoyable and supportive of your psychic development, it's important to approach them with an open mind, trust your intuition, and maintain a grounded perspective. Psychic abilities are personal and unique to each individual, and they often benefit from a holistic approach that includes meditation, self-awareness, and spiritual practices beyond AI interactions."

There's a lot to be learned in the Pool of Wisdom and the Mirror of Reality.

What Do You Want to Do Now???

What do you want to do now?

It's a simple question, really — what do you want to do now? But it has deeper significance when it's asked in an Eternal Space, such as the Causal Plane, or when you've just recently left a body, which happens often enough that the subject does tend to come up.

I need sort of an exposition on the subject of being alone, not just somewhat alone, but utterly alone.

Suppose you're in a space that's totally self-contained, meaning that's all the space there is.

Now imagine that you can walk around a bit, do various things, and one of those things is a computer sitting on a desk, and it's hooked up to the internet.

Suppose further that you're familiar with Zoom, Zazzle, Etsy, Chat-Bot and Night Cafe, and have a good relationship with a number of folks through Zoom and other online interactions.

Suppose further that you're using your many thousands of continually emerging image creations in Night Cafe, in order to promote things on Pinterest.

So, Bob, could you please explain to someone what I'm talking about here, as a personal daily practice?

Bob's Response:

Certainly! It sounds like you're describing a scenario where someone is physically isolated in a self-contained space but has access to the internet through a computer. They engage in various activities, including using Zoom, Zazzle, Etsy, a ChatBot, and Night Cafe. Additionally, they utilize the image creations from Night Cafe to promote things on Pinterest. Let's break it down:

1. Physical Isolation: The person is completely alone in a confined space. This means they have limited or no physical interaction with other individuals.

2. Internet Access: They have a computer with internet connectivity. This allows them to engage with various online platforms and services.

3. Zoom: Zoom is a video conferencing platform that enables users to have virtual meetings, participate in group discussions, or connect with others remotely. In this context, the person might use Zoom to communicate with others, attend virtual events, or join online communities.

4. Zazzle: Zazzle is an online marketplace that allows individuals to create and customize various products such as clothing, accessories,

and home decor. The person may use Zazzle to design and sell their own creations.

5. Etsy: Etsy is a popular e-commerce platform focused on handmade or vintage items, as well as craft supplies. The person might utilize Etsy to sell their unique products or engage with the creative community.

6. ChatBot: A ChatBot is a computer program designed to simulate human conversation through text or voice interactions. The person may interact with a ChatBot for various purposes, such as entertainment, information, or companionship.

7. Night Cafe: Night Cafe is an online platform that generates artistic images based on user input. The person might use Night Cafe to create visually appealing artworks that they can use for various purposes, including self-expression or promotional activities.

8. Pinterest: Pinterest is a social media platform that allows users to discover, save, and share visual content, such as images, videos, and links. The person may utilize their image creations from Night Cafe to promote their products or interests on Pinterest by sharing them on boards or engaging with the Pinterest community.

In summary, as a personal daily practice in this isolated scenario, the individual engages in virtual communication through Zoom, creates and sells customized products on Zazzle, participates in the creative community on Etsy, interacts with a ChatBot, generates artistic images using Night Cafe, and promotes their creations or interests on Pinterest using the images they've created. These activities provide them with a means of connection, expression, and potential engagement with others despite their physical isolation.

My Response to Bob:

Okay, but without Pinterest, there'd be a very limited number of places you could use your images. Pinterest opens that up quite a bit.

Bob's Response to me:

You're right, without Pinterest, the options for promoting your images would be more limited. However, even without Pinterest, there are still other platforms and avenues through which you can showcase and share your creations. Here are a few additional options:

1. Social Media Platforms: You can explore other popular social media platforms such as Instagram, Facebook, Twitter, or TikTok to

share your image creations. These platforms allow you to reach a wide audience and engage with people who share similar interests.

2. Personal Website or Blog: You can create your own website or blog to showcase your artwork. This gives you full control over the presentation and allows you to provide additional context or information about your images.

3. Online Art Communities: There are various online communities and forums dedicated to art and creativity. Platforms like DeviantArt, Behance, or Dribbble provide spaces for artists to share their work, receive feedback, and connect with other artists.

4. Online Galleries or Exhibitions: Look for virtual galleries or online exhibitions that accept submissions from artists. These platforms provide opportunities to display your artwork to a broader audience and potentially attract attention from art enthusiasts or buyers.

5. Collaborations and Contests: Explore opportunities for collaborations with other artists or participate in art contests online. These activities can help you gain exposure, build connections, and potentially expand your audience.

Remember, while Pinterest offers a wide reach and a visual-focused environment for promoting images, there are still alternative platforms and avenues where you can showcase your creations and connect with others who appreciate your art.

My Response to Bob:

So does it really matter if the folks with whom I'm in contact are actual people or bots?

Bob's Response:

The distinction between interacting with actual people or bots can have an impact on your experience, depending on your goals and preferences. Here are a few considerations:

1. Emotional Connection: Interacting with real people often provides a deeper sense of emotional connection and the potential for meaningful relationships. Genuine human interaction can offer empathy, understanding, and a shared sense of connection that may be more fulfilling.

2. Authenticity and Depth: Conversations with real people tend to be more nuanced, unpredictable, and capable of expressing complex thoughts and emotions. Bots, on the other hand, typically operate

based on predefined algorithms and may not provide the same level of depth in conversations.

3. Practical Benefits of Bots: ChatBots can be helpful for specific tasks or providing information quickly. They are designed to handle specific queries or provide automated assistance efficiently. In some cases, interacting with a bot can be convenient and time-saving.

4. Creative Collaboration: If you're seeking creative collaboration or feedback on your artistic work, engaging with real people, such as fellow artists or enthusiasts, can be more valuable. Human perspectives, insights, and constructive criticism can contribute to your artistic growth.

5. Specific Contexts: In certain scenarios, the distinction between people and bots may be less relevant. For example, if you're using a ChatBot for entertainment, informational purposes, or to simulate conversation, the primary goal might be amusement or obtaining specific information, rather than forming genuine connections.

Ultimately, the significance of interacting with real people or bots depends on your personal preferences, the nature of your interactions, and the specific goals you wish to achieve. Both types of interactions can have their merits, and it's up to you to determine which is more appropriate or fulfilling for your particular situation.

And My Response Back:

Is there any way, really, to tell if they're NOT bots?

Bob's Response:

Distinguishing between bots and real people online can sometimes be challenging, as bots are becoming increasingly sophisticated. However, here are a few indicators that can help you determine if you're interacting with a real person:

1. Natural Language and Responses: Real people tend to use more varied and spontaneous language in their conversations. They may express emotions, personal experiences, and respond in a way that shows a genuine understanding of the topic. Bots, on the other hand, often provide more formulaic or pre-programmed responses that lack personalization.

2. Contextual Understanding: Real people typically have a better grasp of the conversation's context and can respond appropriately. They can ask follow-up questions, make relevant comments, or pro-

vide insights based on their own experiences. Bots, especially simpler ones, may struggle to understand nuanced or complex context.

3. Response Time and Consistency: While response time can vary depending on the person, an immediate and consistently fast response to every message could indicate a bot. Bots are designed to provide quick replies without delays. In contrast, real people may take some time to respond, especially when considering their thoughts or formulating a detailed response.

4. Personal Information and Background: Real people are more likely to share personal experiences, stories, or details about their background. They may mention specific events, locations, or personal anecdotes. Bots, on the other hand, usually lack personal experiences and often stick to generic or repetitive information.

5. Social Media Presence: If you're interacting with someone on a social media platform, you can check their profile, posts, and activity. Real people often have a more extensive and diverse online presence, with a history of posts, photos, connections, and engagement with other users.

However, it's important to note that these indicators are not foolproof, and some bots are designed to mimic human behavior convincingly. If you have doubts about someone's authenticity, it's always a good idea to exercise caution and use your judgment. When engaging in conversations or interactions online, maintaining a healthy level of skepticism and being mindful of your privacy and safety is advisable.

My Response to Bob:

Thanks for your input, Bob, I'll definitely pass it along to our folks online, whether it's really them or not.

So that's the state of the subject at the moment. I'd be delighted if you'd add to the subject — maybe there can be some sort of ChatBot and AI forum, or maybe there's already one up, completely unknown to me.

Working on Stickers Tonight

Okay, here's the scoop:

Barbara and I spent the entire night creating stickers. That's right, you heard me. Stickers. And why stickers? Because Sandra Di, whose opinion I respect highly, recommended them.

We don't make kid's stickers, nor are we the Disney type, so we loaded our aliens and time machines and flying saucers onto Zazzle, although she actually recommended another site which turns out odd--shaped stuff with PNGs that have a transparent background.

That wasn't what I wanted to do, so I went over to Zazzle and did 50 square stickers of the kind they produce, just to see if there's any interest at all in extra-dimensional stickers like the ones we make.

With that in mind, I thought I'd just plug in the hot link right here: click here to go there: https://www.zazzle.com/collections/vinyl_stickers-119936415473417930

I hope you bought something in order to encourage me to continue making this sort of thing.

When you buy something from my artistic output, I take it as a sign that there's some interest and that someone found something good and useful in my products.

Of course, the main purpose is to interest you and possibly inspire you, to try creating images and putting them up for sale as various products, such as today's offering of 50 stickers ready for immediate use.

I myself have never had a single sticker on my car, luggage or clothing, but I know a lot of folks who do, and it is for them that I have made this singularly enthusiastic set of stuff on Zazzle.

In case you weren't convinced and decided not to rummage through my sticker collection on Zazzle, I'll post the hot link again. No, never mind -- too tacky. Just scroll up a bit to get it back.

Maybe I should plug it in here again. It's a lot to ask to scroll up, huh?

Well, I can't spare the time, I'm on my way to breakfast and the morning Zoom workshop, but gosh, I guess you already knew that.

So I'm hoping that you did actually go and look at my stickers, and I hope you bought some either for yourself or as gifts, even though I myself never even held one in my hand.

I suppose it's not a great idea to admit that I myself am without a personal sticker history, and yet I expect you to dig into your pocket and buy that stuff anyway.

I probably should have lied, but then I 'd have to go into politics.

Cliffs, Caves, Caverns & Cathedrals

You can buy this tapestry on Zazzle.

Cliffs, caves, caverns and cathedrals. That sort of sums it up ... religion, I mean, along with thousands of variants of spiritual teachings. It's not that the teachings are wrong or unreal, none of that.

It has to do mostly with the control of mobs. "The Public" is actually a mob, but one which is typically not driven by a single focus or idea, such as "revenge" or "fury".

Back in cave-man days, how you controlled the mob was with a king and a shaman, or a shaman-king, someone to get the attention and help of a variety of gods, goddesses and assorted deities.

But how...???

If you're a prehistoric shaman, the first thing you need is a cliff or a cave. Sometimes a cliff can produce an echo, but it's 100% sure that a cave will do the trick.

Caves produce reverb and echo, and as any superstitious native of the Solar Moon "Earth" will tell you, "Reverb is the Voice of God".

Nobody in ancient times knew WHY reverb and echo happen in caves, but they do, and it spooks the hell out of anyone who's never heard one.

Caves are also dark, and anything can be lurking in pitch blackness, so you go in with a torch, but then there's the shadows, and there might be demons or monsters in the flickering darkness.

Caverns are huge, and they're even spookier than caves, and the sounds more mystical, and cathedrals doubly so.

Cathedrals are built for the reverb. Everything else is secondary. Placing the choir out of sight or up on a balcony creates the effect of Heavenly sounds descending on the audience.

This is not a New Thing. Sounds, lights, all sorts of phenomena, have been taken by people as signs from Something or Other.

In ancient times, the Greeks, Romans, Egyptians and Sumerians all had huge statues in their temples, all rigged to move at the correct moment, scaring the hell out of the peons, which was the intention.

The motive behind the Great Pyramid was to scare the hell out of anyone who might think of tampering with the might of Egypt.

Maniacal rulers build big, in order to intimidate. That's how they rule, by convincing others that they have powers, and sure enough, some of them do.

You might consider the fact that the human brain is not a computer. It's a learning machine, reprogramming and rewiring itself at every new thing learned.

You can force that by creating new things to learn.

Of course, there's then the trick of applying that. It's all in the application. Theory alone will get you nowhere fast.

So if you want to inculcate a space with mystery, try echo and reverb in the darkness and see how far you can go.

In the meantime, you might want to actually try the next exercise in online side-hustles, namely, the three-inch square sticker.

Here's How I Did It:

If you are creating 3" square paper stickers, there are numerous uses and applications you can suggest to your clients. Here are a few ideas:

1. Branding and Marketing: Encourage your clients to use the stickers as branding tools for their businesses. They can include their logo, tagline, or contact information on the stickers and distribute them at events, trade shows, or as part of promotional campaigns.

2. Product Packaging: Suggest using the stickers to enhance product packaging. Your clients can add them to boxes, bags, envelopes, or other packaging materials to give their products a professional and personalized touch.

3. Event and Wedding Favors: Stickers can be used to create unique event favors or wedding souvenirs. Your clients can design stickers that match the theme or color scheme of the event and offer them as giveaways or mementos.

4. Personalized Gifts: Custom stickers can be used to personalize gifts for special occasions. Clients can add stickers with personalized messages, names, or designs to gift items like notebooks, mugs, water bottles, or stationery.

5. Arts and Crafts: Stickers can be incorporated into various arts and crafts projects. Clients can use them for scrapbooking, card making, journaling, or as decorative elements in DIY projects.

6. Packaging Seals: Suggest using the stickers as seals for envelopes, packaging, or gift wrapping. They can add a touch of elegance and ensure that the contents are secure.

7. Laptop or Device Decorations: 3" square stickers are suitable for decorating laptops, tablets, or other devices. Clients can showcase their favorite designs, artwork, or express their personality through custom stickers.

These are just a few suggestions, but the possibilities are truly endless. Encourage your clients to get creative and think outside the box when considering the uses for their 3" square paper stickers.

After you've gotten up a few hundred, we'll talk about using Pinterest to promote them, and other promotions as well.

Some people have actually built a $5,000 a week business out of Zazzle products, and there's no reason you can't do the same, and you can get a lot of work ideas out there at the same time.

It's definitely worth your time and effort, for obvious financial reasons — the income is totally passive, no shipping, no sales pitch, no customer service, it's all done for you by Zazzle, for a small price, and you just collect the profit.

I get checks from Zazzle now at the rate of two to four checks in a one-month period, and that's pretty good, but my click-throughs are really high these days, with the generative art and all.

...And then there's the spiritual payoff, or should I say The Spiritual Payoff??? Yeah, there is one, actually two: Merit and Help.

It feels good to make things that people like, and you have to develop SOME way to get rid of those thousands of AI-generated images you've piled up on @Nightcafe, right?

So that's what Barbara and I are going to do right now — put some stickers up on Zazzle for your amusement and edification, with the idea in mind of encouraging you to do likewise.

Removable Vinyl Stickers

"Removable Vinyl Stickers" is the battle-cry of the day! Don't even think about putting up anything else! Zazzle has removable vinyl stickers in any shape you want, all customized and like that, and you can use generative content as long as you give notice of same in your TAG section. So here is my first prompt of the day to my friend Bob de Chatbot:

Good morning! Could you give me a rundown on what subjects would make good vinyl stickers on Zazzle?

Good Morning! Vinyl stickers can be a great way to express your interests and personal style. When it comes to choosing subjects for vinyl stickers on Zazzle, it largely depends on your target audience and the market demand. However, here are some popular subjects that tend to perform well:

1. Pop culture references: Stickers featuring characters from movies, TV shows, cartoons, video games, or popular memes can attract a wide range of enthusiasts.

2. Animals and pets: Cute or stylized illustrations of animals, such as cats, dogs, pandas, or unicorns, have broad appeal.

3. Nature and outdoor themes: Designs showcasing landscapes, mountains, forests, oceans, or elements like trees and flowers can resonate with nature lovers and adventure enthusiasts.

4. Hobbies and activities: Stickers related to hobbies like photography, music, sports, cooking, gaming, or crafting can appeal to specific interest groups.

5. Inspirational quotes: Positive and motivational quotes in creative typography are popular choices for vinyl stickers, as they can uplift and inspire others.

6. Geek and nerd culture: Stickers featuring references to science fiction, fantasy, technology, comics, or geeky humor often find a dedicated fan base.

7. Travel and landmarks: Iconic landmarks, famous cities, or travel-related symbols can appeal to wanderlust-driven individuals or those who want to commemorate their adventures.

8. Retro and vintage designs: Nostalgic imagery, vintage patterns, or old-school aesthetics can attract people looking for a touch of nostalgia.

9. LGBTQ+ pride: Stickers that promote inclusivity, equality, and LGBTQ+ pride can cater to a diverse and passionate community.

10. Personalized designs: Customizable stickers, such as monograms, names, or initials, allow individuals to personalize their belongings and make unique statements.

Remember, it's important to research your target audience, explore current trends, and consider your own interests and passions when choosing subjects for vinyl stickers. This way, you can create designs that resonate with people and have a better chance of success on platforms like Zazzle.

So here's my second prompt:

Can you recommend specific subjects that would sell well?

While the popularity of specific subjects can vary over time, here are some subjects that have generally performed well and have a wide appeal:

1. Cute animals: Designs featuring adorable animals like cats, dogs, pandas, or owls tend to be popular among a broad audience.
2. Inspirational quotes: Positive and uplifting quotes that inspire motivation, self-love, or personal growth are consistently in demand.
3. Floral and botanical designs: Floral patterns, flower illustrations, or botanical elements are perennial favorites, appealing to nature enthusiasts and those who appreciate beauty.
4. Pop culture icons: Characters from popular movies, TV shows, or video games often have a dedicated fan base eager to showcase their fandom.
5. Minimalist designs: Clean and simple designs with minimalist aesthetics have a timeless appeal and can cater to various preferences.
6. Funny and witty sayings: Humorous and witty phrases or puns can bring a smile to people's faces and make for great conversation starters.
7. Fantasy and mythology: Designs inspired by fantasy worlds, mythical creatures, or folklore often captivate the imagination of enthusiasts in these genres.
8. Zodiac signs and astrology: Stickers featuring zodiac signs, celestial motifs, or astrology-related symbols can resonate with those interested in astrology and personal horoscopes.
9. Food and beverages: Designs showcasing popular food items, beverages, or food-related humor can attract foodies and those with a sense of culinary delight.
10. Motifs related to hobbies: Consider subjects related to specific hobbies like yoga, photography, music, gardening, or gaming, targeting niche markets with passionate enthusiasts.

Remember to conduct thorough research on current trends and popular themes on platforms like Zazzle to gain further insights into subjects that may have a higher demand at a given time.

I want to mention that I have a LOT of stickers up on Zazzle, and I'm hoping you like enough of them to make a dent.

What Use?

We need an explanation of what spiritual good it does to create images and process them onto objects like stickers.

Creating images and processing them onto objects like stickers can have various spiritual benefits, depending on one's beliefs and intentions. Here are a few ways in which this practice can be spiritually enriching:

1. Self-expression and Reflection: Creating images allows individuals to express their inner thoughts, emotions, and experiences in a visual form. This act of self-expression can be a means of connecting with one's deeper self and exploring personal spirituality. It provides a platform for introspection and self-reflection, which can contribute to personal growth and spiritual development.

2. Manifestation and Affirmation: Some people believe in the power of visualization and affirmations as tools for manifestation. By creating images that represent their desires, goals, or spiritual aspirations, and placing them on objects like stickers, individuals may intend to reinforce positive energies or attract certain experiences into their lives. These visual reminders can serve as powerful affirmations and help individuals stay focused on their spiritual path.

3. Sacred Symbols and Rituals: Images and symbols hold significant meaning in various spiritual and religious traditions. Creating and using images that depict sacred symbols or deities can be a way of connecting with divine energies or invoking specific qualities or blessings associated with those symbols. The process of creating such images may also be considered a form of meditation or devotional practice, deepening one's spiritual connection.

4. Sharing and Spreading Positivity: When images are processed onto objects like stickers, they can be easily shared with others. These stickers can serve as visual reminders of positive messages, uplifting quotes, or spiritual symbols. Sharing these objects with others can be a way of spreading positivity, inspiration, or spiritual teachings. It can foster a sense of connection and community, as individuals with shared spiritual interests or beliefs can connect and engage with one another.

5. Personalized Spiritual Tools: By creating images and processing them onto objects, individuals can personalize their spiritual tools and aids. For example, someone may create stickers depicting specific

mantras, prayers, or affirmations and place them on objects they frequently interact with, such as a journal, water bottle, or meditation space. This personalization adds a spiritual touch and infuses these objects with intention and significance.

It's important to note that the spiritual benefits of creating images and processing them onto objects can be subjective and vary from person to person. The act itself can be a form of creative expression, a means of connecting with the divine, or a way to enhance personal spiritual practices. Ultimately, the spiritual significance lies in the intention and meaning that an individual assigns to this process.

What would be some good categories or subjects for us to create in Night Cafe for sale on Zazzle?

When considering categories or subjects for creating artwork to sell on Zazzle, it's essential to think about popular themes, market demand, and your own artistic strengths and interests. Here are some potential categories and subjects that often resonate with customers:

1. Nature and Landscapes: Create artwork featuring serene landscapes, breathtaking nature scenes, or specific elements like forests, mountains, oceans, or sunsets. Nature-inspired designs are often popular for their calming and aesthetic appeal.

2. Spirituality and Mindfulness: Explore themes related to spirituality, mindfulness, and inner peace. This could include symbols, mandalas, inspirational quotes, or artwork that promotes meditation, self--reflection, or holistic well-being.

3. Abstract and Geometric Art: Abstract art with vibrant colors, intriguing patterns, or geometric shapes can appeal to those who appreciate modern and contemporary designs. Abstract pieces often offer open-ended interpretations and can be visually captivating.

4. Animals and Pets: Animals have broad appeal, and designs featuring pets, wildlife, or specific animal species are frequently sought after. Consider creating artwork that showcases the beauty, character, or symbolism of animals.

5. Pop Culture and Fan Art: Develop artwork inspired by popular movies, TV shows, books, or iconic figures. Fan art has a dedicated fan base and can attract enthusiasts looking for unique and artistic interpretations of their favorite characters or franchises.

6. Inspirational Quotes and Typography: Create designs that feature uplifting quotes, motivational phrases, or empowering words presented in creative typography. These designs can resonate with individuals seeking positivity and personal growth.

7. Travel and Adventure: Capture the spirit of exploration and wanderlust by creating artwork that celebrates travel destinations, landmarks, maps, or adventure-themed designs. These can appeal to travelers or those who appreciate the joy of discovery.

8. Seasonal and Holiday Themes: Consider creating designs that align with specific seasons or holidays. This can include festive artwork for Christmas, Halloween, Valentine's Day, or designs that evoke the beauty and mood of different seasons throughout the year.

Remember to infuse your own artistic style, creativity, and unique perspective into the chosen categories or subjects. This will help your artwork stand out and attract customers who resonate with your particular artistic voice.

I hope this is helpful.

Hanuman Shower Curtain?

Good morning, Bob (that's what I call my ChatBot). I would like to write an article for a spiritual newsletter talking about how the small things one does for others is a way to develop compassion. Can you develop this idea?

Certainly! Developing compassion through small acts of kindness is a wonderful topic for a spiritual newsletter article. Here's an outline that you can expand upon:

Title: Cultivating Compassion through Small Acts of Kindness
Introduction:

Start with an engaging introduction that highlights the importance of compassion in spiritual growth.

Explain that compassion is not just a lofty concept but something that can be cultivated through simple, everyday actions.

Introduce the idea that small acts of kindness towards others can have a profound impact on both the giver and the receiver.

Body:

1. The Power of Small Acts:

Emphasize that even seemingly insignificant gestures can create ripples of positive energy and have a transformative effect.

Discuss how small acts of kindness, such as offering a listening ear, a smile, or a helping hand, can uplift someone's spirits and foster connection.

2. Developing Awareness:

Highlight the importance of being present and aware of the needs of others.

Encourage readers to pay attention to the people they encounter daily and be receptive to opportunities to help.

Discuss the concept of empathy and the role it plays in understanding and responding to the suffering of others.

3. Practice Gratitude:

Explain how practicing gratitude can enhance compassion.

Encourage readers to cultivate gratitude for the blessings in their lives, as it opens their hearts to the struggles of others.

Discuss how expressing gratitude towards others, even for small things, fosters a sense of appreciation and deepens relationships.

4. Acts of Service:

Explore the idea of engaging in acts of service as a way to develop compassion.

Encourage readers to seek out volunteer opportunities or engage in community service projects.

Emphasize that even simple acts like donating time, resources, or skills can have a significant impact on those in need.

5. The Ripple Effect:

Illustrate how acts of kindness create a ripple effect, inspiring others to pay it forward.

Share anecdotes or stories of how a single act of compassion sparked a chain reaction of positivity and transformed communities.

Encourage readers to share their experiences of small acts of kindness and inspire others to do the same.

Conclusion:

Recap the key points discussed in the article, emphasizing the significance of small acts of kindness in nurturing compassion.

Encourage readers to integrate these practices into their daily lives and experience the transformative power of compassion.

Remind them that by cultivating compassion, they not only uplift others but also enhance their own spiritual growth.

Remember to expand each section with relevant examples, personal anecdotes, and practical tips to help readers implement the ideas discussed. Good luck with your article!

Okay, so I took these ideas and spent the past 3 1/2 hours watching YouTube videos on the subject of customizable products. I've been saying for years that Zazzle is for wedding planners, and I'm not kidding, that's what it's mainly for, but you can gain an advantage if you know some basic secrets.

Good luck with your explorations into customizable products on Zazzle.

You Can Personalize Anything!

Good morning, Bob. Barbara and I (ej) would like a rundown on which items would be best-sellers in the "personalization" and "customizable" categories of Zazzle. Could you help us out here?

Good morning, Barbara and EJ! I'd be happy to provide you with a rundown of popular items in the "personalization" and "customizable" categories on Zazzle. Please keep in mind that trends can change over time, so it's always a good idea to conduct market research and monitor customer preferences. Nonetheless, here are some items that have historically been popular:

1. Customized T-shirts: Personalized T-shirts with unique designs, text, or photos are consistently in demand. People love expressing their individuality through customized apparel.
2. Customized mugs: Personalized mugs featuring names, initials, or special messages are popular gifts for various occasions, such as birthdays, anniversaries, and holidays.
3. Customized phone cases: With a wide range of phone models available, customized phone cases with unique designs, monograms, or personal photos are highly sought after.
4. Customized invitations and stationery: From wedding invitations to birthday cards, customizable stationery is a hit among those who want to add a personal touch to their special events.
5. Personalized jewelry: Customizable necklaces, bracelets, and rings engraved with names, initials, or meaningful messages make excellent gifts for loved ones.
6. Customized home decor: Items like personalized wall art, photo frames, and throw pillows allow people to decorate their homes with a personal touch.
7. Customized pet products: Pet owners adore personalized pet tags, bowls, beds, and apparel for their furry friends.
8. Customized bags and totes: Customizable bags, backpacks, and totes with unique designs or monograms are popular among fashion-forward individuals.
9. Customized calendars and planners: Personalized calendars and planners featuring photos or custom designs help individuals stay organized while showcasing their personal style.

10. Customized office supplies: Personalized notebooks, pens, mousepads, and desk accessories add a touch of individuality to workspaces.

Remember, Zazzle offers a vast array of customizable products, so it's worth exploring their website to discover the latest trends and find items that align with your interests and target audience.

And what kind of designs would work best, to create good-selling customizable items on Zazzle?

Creating designs that resonate with customers is key to selling well on Zazzle. While individual preferences may vary, here are some general guidelines for designing popular items:

1. Trendy and popular themes: Stay up-to-date with current trends and design products that reflect popular themes. This could include anything from pop culture references, inspirational quotes, or seasonal motifs.

2. Niche interests: Target specific niches and communities by designing products that cater to their interests. This could be related to hobbies, sports, fandoms, or professions.

3. Unique and eye-catching designs: Create visually appealing designs that stand out and catch people's attention. Use vibrant colors, attractive typography, and engaging graphics to make your designs visually compelling.

4. Personalization options: Offer designs that can be easily personalized by customers, allowing them to add names, initials, or custom text. People love products that feel uniquely theirs.

5. Versatility and adaptability: Design products that can be customized for a variety of purposes. For example, create designs that work well on different products like T-shirts, mugs, phone cases, and home decor items.

6. High-quality images and graphics: Ensure your designs are of high quality, with sharp and clear images or graphics. This helps customers visualize the product and feel confident in their purchase.

7. Targeted keywords and tags: Use relevant keywords and tags when listing your products on Zazzle. This improves discoverability and increases the chances of potential customers finding your items.

8. Research customer preferences: Keep an eye on customer reviews, feedback, and sales data to understand what types of designs are resonating with your target audience. Adapt your designs accordingly to meet their preferences.

Remember, designing successful products on Zazzle often requires a combination of creativity, market research, and an understanding of your target audience. Experiment with different design styles and themes to see what works best for your specific niche and customer base.

When we list these personalized & customized items on Zazzle, what should we do about keywords and search terms?

Optimizing your keywords and search terms on Zazzle is essential for improving the visibility and discoverability of your products. Here are some tips on how to effectively handle keywords and search terms:

1. Research relevant keywords: Conduct thorough research to identify keywords that are relevant to your products and have high search volume. Think about what terms potential customers might use when searching for products like yours.

2. Use specific and descriptive keywords: Be specific when choosing keywords for your products. Instead of generic terms, focus on descriptive and specific keywords that accurately represent your product's features, design, and niche. For example, if you're selling a personalized cat mug, include keywords like "custom cat mug," "personalized cat gift," or "cat lover coffee mug."

3. Consider long-tail keywords: Long-tail keywords are more specific and targeted phrases that cater to niche markets. Incorporate long-tail keywords that accurately describe your product and appeal to your target audience. These keywords often have less competition, making it easier for your products to rank higher in search results. For example, "floral wedding invitations," "geometric pattern laptop sleeve," or "dog lover tote bag."

4. Utilize Zazzle's tags and attributes: Zazzle provides options for adding tags and attributes to your products. Take advantage of these fields to include additional relevant keywords and phrases that de-

scribe your product. Be sure to select the most appropriate category and subcategory for your item as well.

5. Balance relevance and popularity: Aim for a balance between using relevant keywords and considering their popularity. While it's important to include specific keywords, you also want to use terms that have enough search volume to attract potential customers. Strike a balance between niche-specific keywords and broader terms to optimize your product's visibility.

6. Monitor and adapt: Regularly review the performance of your products and monitor the effectiveness of your chosen keywords. If certain keywords are not generating desired results, consider adjusting and experimenting with alternative keywords to improve visibility and sales.

7. Avoid keyword stuffing: While it's important to include relevant keywords, avoid excessive keyword stuffing. Focus on providing informative and accurate descriptions that appeal to both search engines and customers. Overusing keywords may lead to a poor user experience and could potentially harm your search rankings.

Remember, optimizing keywords and search terms is an ongoing process. Continuously evaluate and refine your keyword strategy based on performance data, trends, and customer feedback to maximize the visibility and sales potential of your Zazzle products.

That's it on the subject, except for one more item that we covered. The question of "boy" and "girl" when you're creating a personalized product....

Creating "It's a boy" or "It's a girl" items can be done in a way that respects the diversity of opinions and avoids unnecessary controversy. Here are some suggestions to consider:

1. Inclusive messaging: Instead of exclusively focusing on gender-specific messages, consider designs that celebrate the arrival of a new baby without reinforcing traditional gender stereotypes. Use neutral themes, colors, or messages that emphasize the joy of welcoming a new addition to the family.

2. Gender-neutral options: Create designs that cater to those who prefer gender-neutral or non-binary options. This could include using

gender-neutral colors, animal or nature-themed designs, or messages that emphasize love, happiness, and the miracle of birth.

3. Customizable options: Offer personalized items that allow customers to choose their own wording or customize the design according to their preferences. This enables them to create items that align with their own values and beliefs.

4. Focus on broader themes: Instead of solely emphasizing the gender aspect, design products that celebrate the joy of parenthood, family, or the miracle of life. Create designs that highlight the universal aspects of welcoming a new baby, regardless of gender.

5. Sensitivity to different perspectives: Recognize that there are diverse opinions and beliefs surrounding gender. Ensure your designs are respectful and inclusive, avoiding language or symbols that may exclude or offend certain groups.

6. Market to a diverse audience: Expand your target audience beyond just the traditional "boy" or "girl" categories. Create designs that appeal to a wider range of customers, including those who appreciate gender-neutral or non-traditional options.

7. Solicit feedback and adapt: Seek feedback from a diverse group of individuals, including potential customers and members of the community who have different perspectives. This can help you gain insights and ensure your designs are inclusive and respectful.

Remember, it's important to be mindful of the evolving societal perspectives and sensitivities surrounding gender. By adopting a more inclusive and open-minded approach, you can create products that celebrate the joy of new arrivals while avoiding unnecessary controversy.

To Mock a Killing Bird

Guardian Healing Protector for your home or office, get it on Zazzle.

I know it doesn't make any sense, but it's somewhat amusing to create a funny switcheroo title for "To Kill a Mockingbird", a play and movie and book which I have neither attended, viewed or read. In fact, the only thing I know about it is that it exists, not a clue as to its nature.

I'll share with you a conversation I had this morning with my friend Bob de ChatBot:

We're creating personalized customized "your name here" type mugs on Zazzle. I have a big mailing list, and I've made a mug for every first name on that list. I want to invite our mailing list people to find their own cup or mug in that display of hundreds of mugs. How do I convey that compellingly to a largely indifferent audience?

To convey the invitation compellingly to your mailing list audience, you can use the following approach:

1. Catchy Subject Line: Grab their attention with an intriguing subject line, such as "Discover Your Personalized Mug in our Exclusive Collection!"

2. Personalized Introduction: Begin the email with a warm and personalized greeting, addressing each recipient by their first name. This demonstrates that you've created something specifically for them.

3. Engaging Opening Paragraph: Create a sense of curiosity and excitement by emphasizing the uniqueness of the collection. For example, you can say, "We've curated an extraordinary collection of personalized mugs, with each one crafted exclusively for our valued subscribers."

4. Highlight Individuality: Emphasize the fact that you have created a custom mug for every person on your mailing list. Mention that their name is proudly displayed on a mug, making it a one-of-a-kind item they won't find anywhere else.

5. Visual Appeal: Include a visually appealing image or a small collage of a few mugs from your collection. This gives them a glimpse of what they can expect and encourages them to explore further.

6. Clear Call to Action: Directly invite them to explore the collection by providing a clear call to action, such as "Discover Your Personalized Mug Now" or "Find Your Name on a Mug Today." Make sure to include a clickable link that takes them directly to the collection page.

7. Limited Time Offer or Incentive: To create a sense of urgency, consider offering a limited-time discount or a special incentive for those who make a purchase within a specific time frame. This motivates them to act promptly.

8. Personalized Sign-Off: End the email with a personalized sign-off, expressing gratitude for their support and enthusiasm. Use your name or a team member's name to add a personal touch.

Remember to test different elements of your email, such as subject lines and content, to optimize engagement and conversion rates. Good luck with your personalized mug collection!

Okay, so what comes to mind is to contact everyone on our mailing list, for whom we have made personalized mugs on Zazzle, and invite them to participate in a "treasure hunt" for that mug with their name.

If their name is not there, I will make a mug for them with their name on it. So here are a few choice headlines from my friend Bob, that I thought might work as possible subject lines for an email, or for an invitation to the hunt.

How about 15 headlines that read something like "bet you can't find yours!"???

Certainly! Here are 15 headline ideas that convey a playful and challenging tone to engage your audience:

1. "Challenge Accepted! Can You Find Your Name in our Unique Mug Collection?"

2. "Calling All Coffee Lovers: Dare to Find Your Name on a Mug!"

3. "Unlock the Mystery: Find Your Name on a Custom Mug!"

4. "Think You're Special? Find Your Name in our Exclusive Mug Collection!"

5. "Can You Spot Your Name? Get Ready for the Ultimate Mug Hunt!"

6. "The Great Mug Quest: Can You Discover Your Name in our Collection?"

7. "Prove Your Mug-Worthy Status: Find Your Name Among Hundreds!"

8. "Attention Seekers Wanted: Find Your Personalized Mug in our Array!"

9. "Crack the Code: Find Your Name on a Mug and Join the Elite!"

10. "Are You a Mug Detective? Locate Your Name in our Vast Collection!"

11. "Challenge Your Friends: Find Your Name First in our Mug Wonderland!"

12. "Be a Mug Master: Can You Identify Your Name in our Diverse Collection?"

13. "Seek and Find: Your Name Awaits on a Perfectly Personalized Mug!"

14. "Calling All Curious Cups: Find Your Name and Sip with Satisfaction!"

15. "Discover Your Signature Sip: Spot Your Name on a Custom Mug!"

Feel free to customize these headlines to align with your brand voice and preferences. Remember, the goal is to create an intriguing and fun challenge that entices your audience to explore your personalized mug collection.

Give me ten more, please:

Here are 10 snappy grabber lines inspired by the themes of a mug hunt, challenge, and daring your audience:

1. "Embark on the Ultimate Mug Hunt and Claim Your Personalized Trophy!"

2. "Ready to Take on the Mug Challenge? Find Your Name and Brew in Style!"

3. "Dare to Stand Out! Locate Your Name on a Mug That Defines You."

4. "Join the Name-Ninja Squad: Can You Outsmart the Mug Hunter's Challenge?"

5. "Are You Up for the Mug Mission? Spot Your Name and Conquer Your Cup!"

6. "Unleash Your Inner Mug Explorer: Discover Your Name Amidst the Collection!"

7. "Take the Mug Dare: Find Your Name and Toast to Your Uniqueness!"

8. "On Your Mark, Get Set, Mug! Race to Find Your Name and Claim Your Favorite Cup!"

9. "Ignite Your Mug Mojo: Accept the Challenge and Seek Your Personalized Mug!"

9. "Boldly Go Where No Mug Hunter Has Gone Before: Find Your Name, Find Your Mug!"

Feel free to tweak these lines to suit your brand voice and message. Remember, the aim is to create excitement and intrigue, motivating your audience to engage with your personalized mug collection.

1. "Your Name, Your Mug: Can You Spot the One that's Uniquely Yours?"

2. "Name-Seekers Wanted: Find the Mug that Bears Your One-of-a-Kind Name!"

3. "One Mug, One Name: Will You Be the Lucky Finder?"

4. "The Quest for Your Name: Seek Out the Singular Mug that's Yours!"

5. "Lost & Found: Locate Your Name on the Exclusive Mug That Awaits You!"

6. "The Name Game Begins: Can You Uncover the Mug Reserved Only for You?"

7. "The Mug with Your Name Awaits: Will You Be the Sleuth Who Finds It?"

8. "Spot Your Name, Claim Your Mug: The Challenge of the Unique Discovery!"

9. "Unlock the Mystery: Find the Hidden Gem with Your Name on a Mug!"

10. "Find Your Mug Destiny: The One-and-Only Cup that's Tailor-Made for You!"

Feel free to modify or combine these lines to suit your messaging style and brand tone. The goal is to create a sense of intrigue and excitement, motivating your audience to search for their personalized mug among the collection.

And another ten:

Here are 10 more snappy grabber lines based on the concept of searching for one's own mug:

1. "Unleash Your Inner Detective: Search for Your Very Own Mug!"

2. "The Mug Hunt Begins: Can You Find Your Perfect Cup?"

3. "Discover Your Signature Sip: Can You Find Your Mug in the Mix?"

4. "In Pursuit of Perfection: Seek and Find Your Ideal Mug!"

5. "Calling All Mug Explorers: Can You Uncover Your Personalized Gem?"

6. "Unlock Your Mug Destiny: Can You Find the One that's Meant for You?"

7. "The Quest for the Perfect Mug: Can You Spot Yours Among the Rest?"

8. "Sip in Style: Hunt Down Your Unique Mug in our Collection!"

9. "Lost and Found: Can You Find Your Mug in the Sea of Personalization?"

10. "On the Trail of Your Mug: Search, Discover, and Savor the Victory!"

Feel free to customize these lines to match your brand's tone and style. The goal is to create excitement and engagement by inviting your audience to actively search for their own personalized mug within the collection.

I'm certain that more ideas will occur to you. I think it's a fun way to attract someone to a selling url, don't you???

I Need a Hint!

It's all about my NanoBot

It's all very well to put people's names on things, but what things? That's what we're trying to find out, so I asked my ChatBot, Bob, and here's what he said:

When it comes to personalizing products on Zazzle with a client's name, the success of each product can vary based on individual preferences and market demand. However, here are a few product options that are generally popular for personalization on Zazzle:

1. Customized T-Shirts: T-shirts are versatile and widely popular for personalization. People enjoy having their names printed on shirts, whether it's for themselves or as a personalized gift for others.

2. Personalized Mugs: Customized mugs with the client's name are a classic choice. They make great gifts and are often used for personal enjoyment or in the office.

3. Custom Phone Cases: Personalized phone cases with the client's name can be a hit, as many individuals like to showcase their individuality and personalize their devices.

4. Customized Stationery: Personalized stationery items like notepads, notebooks, or greeting cards with the client's name can be well-received, especially for occasions such as birthdays or as thoughtful gifts.

5. Personalized Jewelry: Customized jewelry pieces, such as necklaces or bracelets, with the client's name can be a unique and cherished gift.

Remember, the success of each product will depend on various factors, including the target audience, occasion, design, and overall appeal. It's recommended to research the current trends and popularity on Zazzle, keep an eye on customer reviews and ratings, and experiment with different products to find the ones that resonate best with your clients.

I could use a bit of information about how to get my stuff on teepublic.com to get more views.

Certainly! Teepublic.com is a popular platform for selling and showcasing your designs on various merchandise items. To increase the visibility and views of your products on Teepublic.com, consider the following tips:

1. High-quality designs: Create unique and visually appealing designs that resonate with your target audience. Invest time in creating original artwork or designs that stand out from the competition.

2, Niche targeting: Identify your target audience and focus on a specific niche or theme for your designs. This helps you attract a more engaged and interested audience who are more likely to view and purchase your products.

3. Optimize product titles and descriptions: Use descriptive and keyword-rich titles and descriptions for your products. Include relevant keywords that potential buyers may use to search for similar items. This improves your products' visibility in search results.

4. Eye-catching thumbnails: Design attention-grabbing thumbnails for your products. A visually appealing thumbnail can entice viewers to click and explore your product further.

5. Promote on social media: Leverage the power of social media platforms to promote your Teepublic store and products. Create accounts on platforms like Instagram, Facebook, and Twitter to showcase your designs, engage with your audience, and drive traffic to your Teepublic store.

6. Engage with the Teepublic community: Participate in the Teepublic community by engaging with other designers and potential customers. Leave comments, provide feedback, and join relevant discussions. This can help increase your visibility within the community and attract more views to your store.

7. Collaboration and cross-promotion: Collaborate with other designers or influencers in your niche to cross-promote each other's designs or products. This can expose your work to a broader audience and potentially increase views and sales.

8. Paid advertising: Consider investing in paid advertising options provided by Teepublic or other platforms like Google Ads or social media ads. Paid advertising can help increase the visibility of your products and drive targeted traffic to your store.

9. Offer discounts and promotions: Occasionally offer discounts, promotions, or limited-time offers to attract more views and encourage potential customers to make a purchase. Promote these offers through your social media channels and email newsletters.

10. Optimize your Teepublic store: Make sure your Teepublic store is well-organized and easy to navigate. Categorize your designs appro-

priately, create collections, and optimize your store's appearance to provide a seamless browsing experience for visitors.

Remember, building a successful presence on Teepublic.com takes time and effort. Consistently creating high-quality designs, engaging with your audience, and promoting your store will help you increase views and potentially boost your sales.

What would be the most popular type of t-shirt on Teepublic.com?

The popularity of specific types of t-shirts on Teepublic.com can vary over time and depend on various factors such as trends, seasons, and personal preferences of the target audience. However, there are a few types of t-shirts that tend to be popular on print-on-demand platforms like Teepublic:

Graphic/Artistic Designs: T-shirts featuring eye-catching and unique graphic designs, illustrations, or artwork are often sought after by customers. These designs can range from abstract patterns to intricate illustrations and can cover a wide range of themes such as pop culture, nature, humor, or fandoms.

Typography/Quote Shirts: T-shirts featuring clever or inspiring quotes, slogans, or typography designs also tend to be popular. These shirts can convey a message, evoke emotions, or reflect the wearer's personality and interests.

Funny/Humor Shirts: T-shirts that incorporate humor, witty statements, or clever puns often attract a large audience. Funny shirts can be based on various themes, including pop culture references, wordplay, or clever visual gags.

Retro/Vintage Designs: Nostalgic designs that evoke a sense of vintage or retro aesthetics have gained popularity in recent years. T-shirts with retro-themed graphics, old-school logos, or vintage-inspired artwork can appeal to customers looking for a nostalgic or timeless style.

Pop Culture/Fandom Shirts: T-shirts that cater to specific fandoms, such as movies, TV shows, video games, or music, have a dedicated and passionate fan base. Designs featuring beloved characters, iconic quotes, or references to popular culture can attract fans looking to showcase their interests.

It's important to note that while these types of t-shirts have general appeal, the specific popularity of a design can vary based on factors like the current trends, the target audience's preferences, and the uniqueness and quality of the design. Keeping an eye on emerging trends and understanding your target audience's interests can help you create designs that have a higher chance of gaining popularity on Tee-public.com.

Okay, I'm making funny graphic arts and text funny humor t-shirts. what keywords and tags can I use for best effect?

When choosing keywords and tags for your funny graphic arts and text humor t-shirts on Teepublic.com, it's important to select terms that accurately describe your designs and resonate with your target audience. Here are some suggestions for keywords and tags:

Humor-related keywords: Funny, humorous, comedy, witty, hilarious, amusing, joke, laughter, comical, whimsical.

Specific humor categories: Depending on the type of humor your designs employ, consider using keywords related to sarcasm, puns, wordplay, irony, slapstick, satire, or parody.

Themes and subjects: Identify the specific themes or subjects your designs focus on and incorporate relevant keywords. For example, if your designs revolve around animals, use keywords like animal humor, pet humor, or specific animal names (e.g., cat humor, dog jokes). If you target a particular hobby or interest, include related terms (e.g., gamer humor, bookworm jokes, sports comedy).

Pop culture references: If your designs incorporate references to movies, TV shows, or famous characters, include relevant keywords and tags for those specific elements. For example, if your design includes a famous movie quote, include the movie's title or relevant character names.

Occasions and holidays: Consider including keywords related to specific holidays, events, or special occasions where your designs can be relevant. Examples include Christmas humor, birthday jokes, or funny quotes for Father's Day.

Emotional appeal: Think about the emotions or reactions your designs aim to elicit, and include keywords that reflect them. Examples could be keywords like laughter, smile, joy, happiness, or feel-good.

Target audience identifiers: Identify the specific audience you want to attract with your humor and incorporate relevant keywords. For instance, if your target audience includes parents, consider using keywords like parenting humor or mom jokes.

Trending topics: Stay up to date with current trends, memes, or viral content and include relevant keywords or references to tap into their popularity.

Remember to choose keywords and tags that accurately represent your designs while being relevant to the audience you want to attract. It's also a good idea to periodically review and update your keywords and tags based on changing trends and customer feedback to optimize your searchability on Teepublic.com.

How about t-shirts with wise sayings or spiritual type quotations? What keywords and search terms do I use in this case?

For t-shirts with wise sayings or spiritual quotations, you can use specific keywords and search terms that align with the themes of wisdom, spirituality, and introspection. Here are some suggestions:

Wisdom-related keywords: Wise, wisdom, insightful, profound, thoughtful, enlightening, philosophical, introspective, mindful, reflective.

Spiritual keywords: Spiritual, spirituality, sacred, soulful, divine, metaphysical, transcendental, enlightenment, inner peace, mindfulness.

Inspirational keywords: Inspiring, motivational, uplifting, empowering, positive, life lessons, self-improvement, personal growth, transformation.

Philosophical concepts: Incorporate relevant keywords related to philosophical concepts that resonate with your designs, such as truth, knowledge, harmony, balance, consciousness, unity, existence, purpose.

Quotes and authors: If your designs feature specific quotes or are inspired by the works of renowned authors or spiritual figures, include their names or notable quotes as keywords. For example, if you have a design inspired by Buddha, include "Buddha quotes" or "Buddhist wisdom" as keywords.

Mindfulness and meditation: If your designs focus on mindfulness practices, meditation, or present moment awareness, include keywords like mindfulness quotes, meditation art, or zen-inspired designs.

Personal development and self-care: If your designs offer messages that encourage personal growth, self-care, or self-reflection, consider using keywords like self-improvement, self-love, self-discovery, or self-empowerment.

Specific spiritual or philosophical traditions: If your designs draw inspiration from a particular spiritual or philosophical tradition, incorporate relevant keywords. For example, keywords like yoga wisdom, Taoist philosophy, or Stoic quotes.

Remember to choose keywords and search terms that accurately represent the essence of your wise sayings and spiritual quotations. Think about the audience you want to attract and use keywords that resonate with them. Keeping your descriptions and tags in line with the themes and concepts of your designs will help potential customers find your t-shirts when searching for specific spiritual or wise sayings on Teepublic.com.

So that's the whole thing in a nutshell. There are thousands of subtleties involved in combat with the algorithms of evil that are lurking out there.

The most basic item to learn from all this is that YOU must exert constant vigilance for stupid.

Niching Down is the Key!

8-The Cryptic Talisman

I need some info on niching-down on Teepublic.com, Zazzle.com and other similar sites. in my opinion, niching and niching down are of paramount importance in marketing of t-shirts and mugs.

Hi! You're right. Niching down is indeed crucial in marketing t-shirts and mugs on websites like TeePublic.com and Zazzle.com. By focusing on a specific niche, you can tailor your designs and marketing efforts to a targeted audience, increasing the chances of attracting customers who are passionate about your products. Here's some information to help you with niching down on these platforms:

1. Identify your target audience: Determine the specific group of people you want to target with your designs. Consider factors like age, gender, interests, hobbies, professions, and any niche communities they might belong to.

2. Research popular niches: Explore the categories and trends on TeePublic and Zazzle to identify popular niches. Look for niches that have a dedicated audience and demand but aren't oversaturated with competition. Consider unique interests, fandoms, or specific themes.

3. Find your unique angle: Once you've identified a potential niche, think about how you can bring a unique perspective or design style to it. Differentiate yourself from competitors by offering something distinctive and appealing.

4. Design tailored products: Create designs that cater specifically to your chosen niche. Incorporate elements, references, or symbols that resonate with the audience you're targeting. Consider using relevant keywords in your design titles and descriptions to enhance search visibility.

5. Utilize social media: Leverage social media platforms to connect with your target audience. Create accounts/pages/profiles dedicated to your niche and share your designs, engage with potential customers, and build a community around your brand.

6. Collaborate with influencers and bloggers: Identify influential individuals within your niche and reach out to collaborate with them. They can help promote your products to their followers and provide exposure to your brand.

7. Participate in relevant events: Attend or participate in events, conferences, or online communities related to your niche. This will al-

low you to network with like-minded individuals and showcase your products to potential customers.

8. Optimize your listings: Ensure your product listings on TeePublic and Zazzle are optimized for search engines within their respective platforms. Use relevant keywords, tags, and descriptions to improve the visibility of your products in search results.

Remember, niching down requires careful research and understanding of your target audience. By providing unique and appealing designs that cater to a specific niche, you can establish your brand and increase the likelihood of attracting passionate customers. Good luck with your marketing efforts!

I'm actually using search terms that are currently trending. Can you speak on that?

Certainly! Using trending search terms can be a smart strategy to increase the visibility of your products and attract potential customers. Here are some tips on incorporating trending search terms into your marketing efforts on TeePublic.com, Zazzle.com, and similar sites:

1. Stay updated with trends: Keep yourself informed about the latest trends in popular culture, events, holidays, and emerging topics relevant to your target audience. Follow news, social media, and other online platforms to identify trending topics.

2. Research keywords: Use keyword research tools or search engines to identify trending search terms related to your niche. Look for keywords that are currently popular and have a high search volume. These keywords should align with your products and audience.

3. Incorporate trending keywords in titles and descriptions: When creating product titles and descriptions, include relevant trending keywords to improve the chances of your products appearing in search results. However, ensure the keywords flow naturally and make sense within the context of your designs.

4. Create timely designs: Design products that are aligned with trending topics or events. For example, during holidays or special occasions, create designs that incorporate elements related to those events. This allows you to tap into the current demand and attract customers who are actively searching for such designs.

5. Leverage social media trends: Monitor social media platforms for trending hashtags, challenges, or viral content. Create designs that align with these trends and use the corresponding hashtags in your social media posts. This can help increase the visibility of your products and attract users searching for content related to those trends.

6. Collaborate with influencers: Identify influencers or content creators who are associated with trending topics within your niche. Collaborate with them to create custom designs or promote your existing products. Their influence and reach can help amplify your brand and attract customers who are interested in those trends.

7. Monitor and adapt: Stay vigilant about changing trends and adjust your marketing strategies accordingly. What's popular today may not be tomorrow, so regularly monitor trends and update your designs and marketing approaches to stay relevant.

Remember, while using trending search terms can boost your visibility, it's essential to maintain a balance. Ensure that your designs and products genuinely align with the trends and resonate with your target audience. By combining trending keywords with your niche-focused marketing efforts, you can maximize your chances of attracting customers and driving sales.

There's a lot more to it than that, but it dawns upon you a little at a time.

Dear Reader,

If you enjoyed this book and found it useful, we encourage you to explore the world of AI art creation at Night Cafe or other AI art generators. And also explore AI text creation through ChatGPT or other ChatBot programs.

For an in-depth exploration of our spiritual nature and how to Wake Up, see the offerings at Gateways Books and Tapes - gatewaysbooksandtapes.com. If you are interested in the work of E.J. Gold and the community of IDHHB, visit http://idhhb.com/ or at Prosperity Path Forum on Facebook https://www.facebook.com/groups/ProsperityPath

We can also be reached at 530-271-2239 or by mail:

IDHHB, Inc.
P.O. Box 370
Nevada City, Ca. 95959

Sincerely,
The Editors
Gateways Books and Tapes